The Houses of Mankind

Colin Duly

T&H

THAMES AND HUDSON

The illustration on the cover is of a *haus tambaran* from the Sepik
River district of New Guinea

© Blacker Calmann Cooper Ltd, 1979
This book was designed and produced by
Blacker Calmann Cooper Ltd, London

Filmset by Southern Positives and Negatives (SPAN), Lingfield,
Surrey
Printed in Spain by Heraclio Fournier, S.A.

Library of Congress Catalog card number: 78–55036

Contents

Introduction 5

Africa 29

The Americas 35

Oceania 71

Eurasia 85

Bibliography 94
Acknowledgements and list of illustrations 94
Index 95

Tlingit

Kwakiutl
Blackfoot Ojibwa
Mandan Ottawa
Crow Iroquois

Pawnee

Yokuts

Zuñi

Maya

Panare

Witoto
Barasana
Yagua

Inca

Bororo

Ona

Lapp

Anatolia

El Oued

Madan

Assa

Tuareg
Songhai Nubians Bedouin
Dogon Meidob Barat
Fulani
Hausa Massa Toda Nio
Shenge Lake Ganvié
Tiv Galla
Konso
Rwanda
Maasai

Bantu

Zulu

Introduction

Map showing locations of tribes

When André Gide walked among the villages of the Massa, on the banks of the Logone which separates the African states of Chad and Cameroun, he was astonished that 'the few rare travellers who have spoken of this country and of its villages have only thought fit to mention their "strangeness". The Massas' hut, it is true, resembles no other; but it is not only strange; it is *beautiful*.' There have been other sympathetic accounts of aboriginal domestic architecture, but disparaging accounts far outweigh these. The notion of the 'primitive hut' is commonly introduced as a hazy stereotype in many standard works of architectural history, as the supposed link with 'the cave' in the lineal ascent towards today's cityscape. In other disciplines — notably biology, in which the theory of evolution was first propounded — this conception of unilineal change has long since lost intellectual credence. Wider and more systematic gathering of information has led to the development of more rigorous systems of classification, which in turn reveal 'change' as a very much more complex phenomenon.

The present work is not concerned with 'change', or at least it is not concerned with tracing our western architectural heritage backwards through Palladian, Greco-Roman and Mesopotamian influences until we reach a single point in the Palaeolithic past. The development of present-day house forms all around the world cannot be told as a single story; it is, rather, a mosaic, and the elucidation of origins is not our concern here. There is tremendous variability in the rates of change of house form: a contemporary farmer's house of the Tigre of Ethiopia shows a striking likeness to a clay model of a house found nearby but made 1,500 years before. In Anatolia, contemporary houses (plate 3) differ only in detail from those excavated by Mellaart at the Anatolian Neolithic site of Çatal Hüyük, and dating from 6,500 BC. In other communities, changes in the circumstances of life, livelihood or beliefs may be breathtakingly rapid. We would expect architecture, as one of the more visible aspects of material culture, directly to reflect these influences; the Yukpa house (of which the example in plate 1 is walled with coloured cans) has changed out of recognition in a single generation under missionary influence. But new materials do not always have this effect. The classic example is the Greek Doric order, the shape and characteristics of which were retained exactly throughout the two centuries during which the original wooden columns evolved into stone. The Buryat Mongols (plate 88) have used plastic sheeting as a replacement of the traditional felt covering to their *ger*, with no change in external form whatsoever (the significance of changes in the disposition of things within the tent will be discussed later).

1. A house in a mission settlement in the Sierra de Perija region of western Venezuela, inhabited by the Yukpa Indians. It is common for missionaries and other non-Indians to encourage the building of walls to ensure European standards of privacy and sexual decorum; that end has been achieved in this case by fabricating walls out of surplus cans from a local dried-milk factory.

2. The façade and details of a sacred house built over water, from Dorey, New Guinea. The painting was made on Dumont D'Urville's Pacific voyage of exploration aboard the *Astrolabe*, which lasted three years from 1825. Carving of house posts is very widespread throughout Melanesia. Note that the central supports are of female, the peripheral supports of male figures; usually, the female is excluded from any association with religion in this area.

When the economy is just about at subsistence level, and the tribe has little contact with other cultures, we generally find that, unlike our own society, it rarely values innovation and novelty, rather regarding them as undesirable or even dangerous. The force of tradition provides the stabilizing element binding one generation to another.

The house plays an intermediary role between man and his world, and everywhere deserves recognition as a powerfully revealing cultural and aesthetic phenomenon. There are some who might argue that none of the examples in this book deserves the description 'architecture', and that that term is an accolade awarded to outstandingly important and impressive buildings. Our concern in this book is with the communicative significance

3. An East Anatolian village near Erzurum, Turkey. Rectangular houses of mud brick reinforced with timber, with flat roofs covered in packed clay, follow a pattern of great antiquity in this region of the Near East. Structures from the Neolithic site of Çatal Hüyük differ only in detail from the contemporary example illustrated. The stacks of dried cow-dung are used for fuel.

of built form, and an open mind as to what constitutes architecture is more appropriate. That architectural writers have neglected tribal domestic building is, however, understandable; the artifacts are generally restricted to the country of origin and make difficult museum pieces. More importantly, if we are to look objectively at aboriginal buildings we must step outside the tradition within which we are used to judging our own indigenous buildings. This is the tradition of the 'edifice complex', the concern of large-scale society with monumental form: the spatial celebration in materials unknown to the tribesman — marble or concrete, steel and glass — of massive concentrations of private, corporate and public wealth and power. Yet even with sensibilities derived from that tradition, the work of some architects is perceived to be alien, sterile and menacing to the individual. Le Corbusier's famous epigram (in *Vers une architecture*, Paris, 1923) that '*Une maison est une machine-*

4. An Australian bark shelter. The aboriginal cultures of Australia are not noted for their material culture, but it does not follow that these are 'simple' societies in all respects. The kinship systems and languages of native Australians are in many cases of enormous complexity and sophistication.

5. A longhouse of the Iban at Long Lenai, Tutoh River, Sarawak, on the island of Kalimantan (Borneo). Among the Iban generally the longhouse is synonymous with the village; it can be as long as 1,000 feet with as many as 500 inhabitants. Raised on massive ironwood pillars, and built of ironwood planks, these houses are immensely durable.

à-habiter' – 'A house is a machine for living' – is a stimulating prescription for an architect with breadth and sensitivity, but there is a danger that if the building's functions are too narrowly defined, the relation between the man and the machine will be an uncomfortable one. This is where the tribal builder can teach us important lessons, for while the 'noble savage' is a myth, he is 'noble' inasmuch as he is never oppressed or cowed by the structures he creates; they are generally built on a human scale by human skills for human needs.

The importance of the topic of the 'human scale' of tribal houses demands that we should spend a little time examining what the phrase implies. The astute reader might conclude from the examples given here that aboriginal man sells himself short as far as housing space is concerned. Even very large structures, such as the longhouse of the Iban (plate 5), turn out to be divided into

quite small individual compartments; the single building may house an entire village, as in parts of Amazonia. From a look at the compact Dogon compound (plate 6), or almost any structure that is required to be mobilized (the Buryat *ger*, plate 88, or the Blackfoot tepee, plate 58), we might well conclude that tribal man is the victim of stressful overcrowding. The notion of over-crowding cannot simply be measured by the number of individuals sharing a house; instead it is a social and psychological concept linked to the culturally transmitted idea of 'privacy', itself a complex bundle of phenomena and meanings. The detailed examination of these concepts by writers such as Edward T. Hall and Erving Goffman has clearly demonstrated that ideas of personal space and orientation run very deep. Obviously, personal space requirements extend beyond the volume of air displaced by one's body; it is as if our bodies are surrounded by invisible 'bubbles' of

6. A Dogon man in the courtyard of a typical compound. His personal granary is in the background.

7. An aerial view of a Madan settlement in the marshlands of the Tigris and Euphrates, Iraq. Each house is built on a small island of rushes and mud and has its own buffalo paddock. The marshes cover about 60,000 square miles.

personal (and portable) territory. The size, shape and resilience of these imaginary bubbles are culturally learned, and change their shape depending on our definition of the relationship before us – be it intimate, personal, formal or public (between strangers). These 'bubbles' vary widely between cultures, of course; the togetherness congenial to an Arab may well be interpreted as an offensive

8. The framework of an unfinished *Dawi* or men's ceremonial house, from the Purari delta region of New Guinea. The gable ends of these cathedrals of bamboo can be eighty feet high.

invasion of bodily territory by the 'cold' European. It is possible that our aesthetic sense of balance, proportion, scale, indeed our notions of the 'correct' relationship of structure to man and structure to environment, have their source in these lowly, everyday interactions. It may be tautologous to claim that tribal man builds structures which suit his habits in their use of space; the presence of more spacious secondary structures on the other hand (such as the club-houses of New Guinea, plates 8, 72) persuades us that it is not a *technical* inability to build on a more expansive scale that denies tribal man his 'basic needs' of space and privacy. Rather, we should conclude that the relationship between building effort and requirements of personal space is neatly judged. Massive forms usually derive from the quite separate needs to express monumentality or prestige. In the case of the spiritually inspired structure, it would be an act of impiety to count the cost of construction; the other common 'hyperstructure' of tribal man, the chief's house, has to incorporate the imperatives of social distance, plus perhaps a little of the feeling of 'accountancy as impiety' attached to the religious building.

Another aspect of the cultures mentioned here is that the triangle with which we are familiar, the A, B and C of Architect, Builder and Consumer, results from the separation of roles, the division into highly specialized functions that both constitutes and promotes modern industrial society. This triangle of interested parties is generally absent from tribal societies; the three functions are compressed, if not to an individual owner-builder, then to a community grouping based on kinship ties or gender rather than occupational specialization. (An exception is provided by the *tohungas*, master craftsmen from Polynesia.) Subsistence economies rarely permit the emergence of full-time building specialists, but in a wide variety of communities the woman's domestic duties include this task, either in construction (Meidob, plate 9) or decoration (Nubians, plate 10). In the case of a co-operating group, money will rarely change hands, but the group for whom the house was built will be expected to reciprocate for the group that provided the labour, and give a feast — perhaps a 'consecration' feast. The obligations built up over this transaction (with the building of the Annamese house, plate 11; or the Assam, plate 91, for example) will bind the community together over time. This close identification with, and community involvement in, the task of providing shelter may account for the purity of style typical of 'face-to-face' societies. Where there is a strong element of tradition, it is a mistake for the builders to deviate from it, and those who do so are likely to suffer the sanctions also laid down by custom.

9. *(Above)* A house of the Meidob, cattle pastoralists living on the margin of the south Libyan Desert in Darfur, Republic of Sudan. They keep large herds of camels, sheep and goats; only the latter are kept near the villages, the other animals being pastured at a distance. This means that the village people need not move over such large distances as the herds, but they shift between as many as six hamlets in a year. The hemispherical timber houses have a framework of cross-beams on four upright posts, on which lean large forked timbers, forming a circle. The wall is built up of progressively smaller branches, and is normally thatched, but the Sahel zone drought of 1968–73 caused the thatching grasses to fail. Meidob houses are made by the women.

10. Birds and acacia trees decorate this house of the Kenuzi Nubians from southern Egypt; decoration, both inside and out, is customarily a woman's job. *(see also plate 20)*

11. An Annamese village near Hanoi in North Vietnam.

The resulting similarity between houses is by no means dull but, rather, is harmonious and attractive; the style is often a vivid response to tribal man's psychic inheritance, of demons, gods, mythical inhabitants from the 'other side', and of ancestors who never 'really' left home. A glimpse at the magnificent polychrome façades or interiors of *haus tambaran* from New Guinea (plates 12, 74 and 75), will convince the reader that the creator of such drama fulfils more than the mere expectations of his fellows in terms of house decoration.

For how much longer we can continue to appreciate these exotic manifestations of tribal art is a question of some urgency. None of us lives in a static, unchanging society, and this includes tribal man. The interpenetration of cultures has never been greater than today; the world appears to shrink as airports spring up from the bush and desert; meanwhile the population continues to expand rapidly. Problems which were once the scholarly preserve of anthropology are now the direct concern of everyone. The very structural changes in western societies which have led to the growing interest in primitive cultures hasten their demise. There have been many tragic encounters between cultures of great technological inequality – the Tasmanian aborigines, the cultures of Tierra del Fuego, the Indians of North and South America and many more besides, all suffered catastrophes in meeting white settlers. Extinction may or may not be brought about intentionally; the result for the tribal peoples concerned has been the same. But there are less unhappy examples of culture contact, when traits are absorbed and become a living part of a culture; influence is reciprocal, and the subsequent growth not only in the cultural repertoire, but in the flexibility with which future changes may be met, makes for a powerful hybrid.

As far as house forms are concerned, it is clear that we cannot stop the clock with a sentimental attachment to the ideal of preservation, conserving those examples which we might consider 'quaint' or even unique. But it is more than an antiquarian interest that compels us to prefer the many examples of functional and beautiful traditional huts to be found in this book to the results of 'third-world housing schemes' which are increasingly numerous. The linear barracks for a newly urbanized proletariat (as exemplified by Soweto, the harsh acronym for the SOuth-WEstern TOwnship of Johannesburg) do not cater for any needs beyond the barest basics required to accommodate an industrial workforce. The urban architect is often faced with the problem of establishing just what people want from their housing: they are not always in a position to press for their requirements to be met, and sometimes

12. A façade from a cult house in the Maprik mountain area of Papua-New Guinea, north of the Sepik River. Throughout the Maprik area, these *haus tambaran* with their stunning representations of ancestor figures and cult spirits dominate the villages in which they are situated.

they are not really capable of articulating what they need and appreciate, although it is essential, from their own point of view, that their needs are expressed. The tribesman on the other hand is probably better able to appreciate built form than urban man, since he is less estranged from the building process.

We should not forget that there are failures as well as successes in tribal architecture. By western standards of comfort and health, the aboriginal house usually falls short. But given the limitations of climate, level of technology, and available materials, we are continually astonished by the ingenuity with which tribal man rises above them. An example of an apparent 'failure', on climatic grounds at least, is the dwelling of the Panare Indians of Venezuela (plate 14), where the huge heat-absorbing thatch, lacking any cross-ventilation, has to be abandoned throughout the summer; but this failure is redeemed by the Panare's use of a simple, light and portable hammock, which permits them to leave camp for the freedom of hunting the forests.

In dealing with the domestic architecture of tribal societies, we are not limited to actual dwellings. 'Domestic' also takes in the special forms associated closely with the primary structure, the house: granaries, storehouses, dormitories, club-houses, houses-of-speech have all been included. Even when the symbol *is* the function, as is the case with monumental architecture, the physical inspiration is often taken from the range of domestic forms. The skills and the style are extrapolations of the skills and style used in building the houses. The designation 'tribal' is problematic. Anthropologists, in attempting to define the term, have exposed the many difficulties of using the tribe as a unit to classify social groups. The term is used here in a loose sense to refer to an autonomous group of people organized primarily by ties of kinship. Further, the group may be internally segmented into lineages or clans; if the clans are ranked, the aristocratic group may produce a leader or chief. The highest level of political organization is almost always below that of a state. In addition, the cultures surveyed in this book generally live by horticulture, pastoralism or a similarly productive hunting activity; only very rarely is there an indigenous system of writing (as among the *women* of the Tuareg of the Sahara), although transcriptions of native tongues in Roman or Arabic script are having increasing and far-reaching consequences.

The central place of the ties of kinship in the composition of the tribe is closely allied to the patterns of domestic space within tribal buildings or communities. The disposition of compounds in West Africa (as among the Songhai of Mali, plate 13; or the Tiv of

13. An aerial view of the Songhai village of Labbézanga, on an island in the Niger River, Mali. Islamic influence is apparent in the square houses; the traditional Songhai dwelling is either round, with a straw roof, or (as in plate 29) an elliptical mat tent. Millet and wild rice granaries coil necklace-like around the houses.

14. A conical house in southern Panare territory, Venezuela. The doorway in the picture is the only opening, apart from a tiny smoke-hole in the roof; the lack of ventilation and the enormous heat-retaining capacity of the palm thatch means that the house is abandoned during the summer months.

15. Millet granaries from Fadiout, coastal Senegal. In societies where the production of food is not yet an industrial process, food itself retains a sacred dimension. Storehouses and granaries are often more elaborate than dwelling-houses (see the display yam-houses of the Trobriand Islanders for an example, in plate 80, or the Maori foodstore, plate 85).

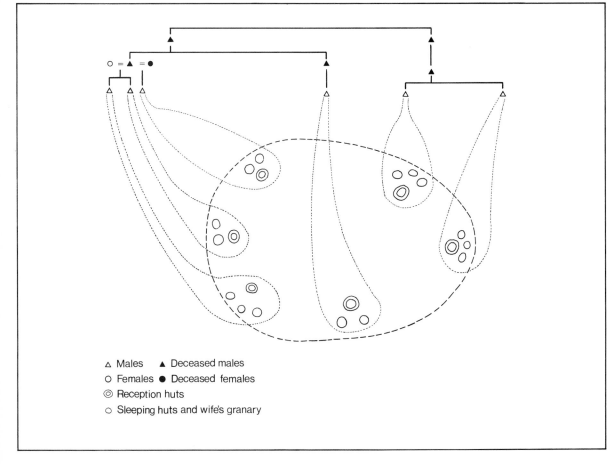

△ Males   ▲ Deceased males
○ Females ● Deceased females
◎ Reception huts
○ Sleeping huts and wife's granary

Nigeria, Fig. 1) can almost be projected from a genealogical chart of the village inhabitants, a kinship scheme writ large. The example of the Bororo of Amazonia (Fig. 2) again demonstrates how intimate kinship connections – in this case relationships between the two halves or moieties of the tribe – can be disrupted through forced changes in village layout. The house in turn is bound up with one part of the kinship network, the family unit. Because tribal houses are usually constructed from permeable materials collected locally, they are in constant need of repair and replacement, in fact, maintenance, rather like the family unit itself. Families are always in a process of change, a continual cycle of expansion and contraction, with ever-changing housing needs. Traditional tribal architecture is more responsive to these changes than more permanent forms; the fact that the house is constantly being 'revised' means that it always suits these changing require-

Fig. 1. A homestead of the Tiv of Nigeria, a tribe with segmentary lineages. The compounds of this tribe without chiefs hold territory according to the relationships to key ancestors. *(after P. Bohannan, Tiv Economy)*

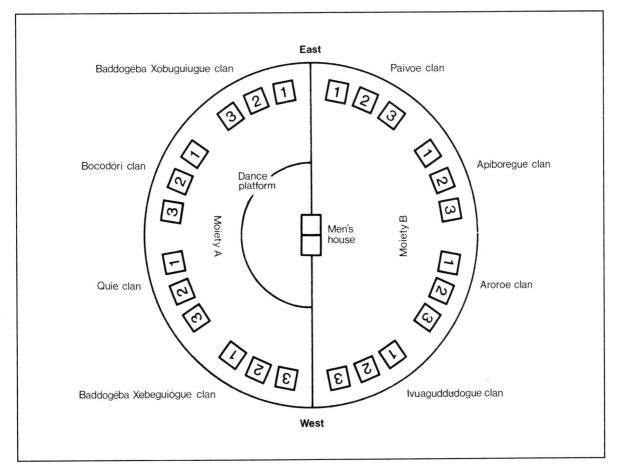

East

Baddogéba Xobuguiugue clan

Paivoe clan

Bocodóri clan

Apiboregue clan

Dance platform

Moiety A

Moiety B

Men's house

Quie clan

Aroroe clan

Baddogéba Xebeguiógue clan

Ivuaguddudogue clan

West

Fig. 2. A plan of a Bororo Indian village of the central Mato Grosso region of Brazil, showing the complex dual organization into clan-houses radiating from a central men's house. Missionaries realized that the most permanent way of converting these people was to make them abandon these concentrically balanced villages and relocate them in houses set in parallel rows. *(after Fr C. Albisetti)*

ments. The fabric of abandoned houses soon disappears, and whilst this may provide a puzzle for the archaeologist in the future, it solves the problem of 'housing blight'; when longevity is required, there is usually an indigenous solution available.

Some key differences between 'tribal' and 'industrial' houses have been touched upon, but if we draw up a checklist of the important distinctions, they seem to lie not in the areas of technique, materials, size or adversity of climate (although tribal societies are over-represented in areas of cruel climate). Instead, the crucial differences seem to be connected with the symbolic aspects of the dwelling, as well as the more communal life of the majority of tribes. The symbolic activities of different tribes vary so widely that it is not possible to offer a general explanation of their effect on house forms: each case must, if it is to explain variety in form, be taken individually. The differentiation in society resulting

16. *(Above)* A Bedouin tent from Qatar in the Arabian Gulf. The inhabitants of *el Bâdia* (the desert) can quickly take advantage of any breeze or protect themselves from wind-blown sand by moving the valance strip from one side to the other; or the tent of woven goat-hair may be closed completely.

17. A fortified house near the Doab Road, Afghanistan, the counterpart of the armed inhabitants of this region, wary of the travellers who pass by between caravanserai.

18. *(Above)* **The large market-town of Suq al 'Ainau in the Barat region of the Yemen Arab Republic. Packed mud construction allows the builders from this region to achieve considerable durability as well as to build many storeys in their town architecture.**

19. **A street-level view of houses from the Barat region of the Yemen Arab Republic. The outlining of the entrance with a powerful design in coloured mud (also used to accentuate the window spaces) and the exploitation of the plastic qualities of packed mud are characteristic of this region of the Yemen.**

from the division of labour and the formation of groups with special skills may to some extent be used as an index of 'primitiveness', and also governs the allocation of domestic space. Various categories of people, goods and activities have different requirements: some or all of the following opposites – people/animals, family/non-family, male/female, interior/exterior, food preparation/food consumption, sleeping/waking and so on – have to be catered for in the domestic domain. These somewhat arbitrary demarcating principles are deeply relevant to the way of life of the people.

Functional specialization in tribal houses may well be less than in western urban houses; in any case the internal organization differs in important ways. Internal structure is strictly prescribed through culture: anything that does not conform is not generally accorded recognition. In certain cultures the family which cooks indoors, or the wife who eats with her husband, or the herdsman who recklessly leaves the young calves outside the house at night obviously know nothing about 'keeping house'.

The particular functional compartments that we take for granted in the European house of today have, like all things taken for granted, a history. The changes in the internal ordering of rooms only became recognizably what they are today as late as the eighteenth century. Yet there are still many rural areas of Europe where cattle occupy the downstairs of a farmhouse, the farmer's sleep being naturally assisted by the knowledge that his working capital is safely deposited in the room below his bed. Philippe Ariès' interesting history *Centuries of childhood* links the 'invention of the child' – the belief that the child was a special type of person rather than a miniature adult – with the emergence of separate bedrooms and nurseries for offspring. In our day, the 'invention of the aged', the result of the change from extended to nuclear family in industrial society, is closely linked with the growth of special settlements for the pensioner (an idea, incidentally, which strikes the tribesman as abhorrent). It is not by chance that the splitting off into small units of the community in our own societies has occurred along with the emergence of enclaves of personal privacy (the dens and studies of suburbia) in our homes. Strictly personal privacy seems to be absent from the houses of tribal mankind, the minimum enclave rarely belonging to a unit smaller than the nuclear family of parents and children.

The aim of this book is simply, and within a limited space, to expose the reader to the character and real diversity of tribal architecture, a refreshing change from the sameness of those parts of the world where the deluge of 'airport plastic' building has taken root. The book is arranged in sections covering the geographical regions: Africa, North and South America, Oceania and Eurasia. This procedure has been followed not because these are the boxes into which humanity naturally falls, but to enable the non-specialist more readily to locate little-known parts of the world, and perhaps to appreciate some of the connections between continental cultures which cannot be explored here. These divisions of the world create unquestionably distinct cradles of culture, but the researcher is constantly surprised by the parallels and contrasts arising from the diffusion of artifacts in the course of trade, or their spontaneous invention. It is hoped that this brief and necessarily highly selective examination of the types of building and their modes of construction and decoration found among some of the indigenous tribal societies of the world, whether living or extinct, will help to reveal that mankind's perception of social relationships is far more significant than either climate or technological skills in deciding how he should enclose, and therefore humanize, the space around him.

Africa

20. *(Left)* Lively paintings on the inner wall of a courtyard house of the Kenuzi Nubians. Colour is also added to the mud-walled exterior, as well as the richly draped interior.

Africa has more distinct peoples among its 250 million inhabitants than any other continent. Indeed, depending on the definition of what constitutes an ethnic unit, there may be as many as five thousand separate tribes, each with their complex but largely unrecorded history. Nowadays, struggles for ethnic identity take place within the context of what were once rather arbitrary national boundaries, established after the colonial 'scramble for Africa' in the nineteenth century, and they continue to pose a challenge to African statecraft.

With more than eleven million square miles, Africa presents a vast range of living conditions. Architecturally speaking, it is rainfall rather than temperature variation which seems to be the significant influence. The range of rainfall levels encompasses both rain forest and desert; outside these two extremes, great problems can also arise from the unpredictability of this life-giving resource: regions suffering drought for months or even years may undergo flash floods from time to time. Native building practices allow for such contingencies, one solution for instance being to use mud or thatch shells, which can easily be replaced.

Far more prevalent than the 'jungle' of popular imagination is savannah – a sparse cover of grass or in more arid regions thorny shrubs, with scattered acacia or baobab trees. More inhospitable are the desert regions – which, perhaps surprisingly, turn out to be far from 'deserted' – the largest of which, the Sahara, is the size of western Europe. Here, tribes lacking the energy-intensive

21. A Zulu kraal from Natal, South Africa. Zulu cosmology is permeated by the notion of the circle. At the height of Zulu power over a century ago kraals could be over a mile in diameter with more than a thousand huts; cattle were kept inside the circle for defensive reasons. Today, with the adoption of mixed farming, stockades have disappeared and cattle-pens have diminished in importance. The grass huts themselves are strikingly similar to those of the related Ngwame Bantu (plate 22).

technology and the corresponding attitudes to control and dominate the environment, compromise with nature in order to live with the desert, and not just in it.

Examining one desert-dwelling tribe, the Tuareg, we find that their accommodation to nature is by means of not one, but many types of shelter. The Tuareg are remarkable, among other things, for the blue veils worn by the men (the women go unveiled, in contrast to Arab practice), and the indigenous script, called *tifinagh*, used only by the women, often to communicate with other women in their travels. The tribe, which consists of several widely dispersed groups, is descended from the Berbers who lived in coastal Libya; the wave of Arab conquests in the seventh century, followed by Bedouin expansion in the eleventh century, forced these people into a life of desert nomadism. Today they inhabit parts of Algeria, Niger, Upper Volta and Mali. Contrary to their austerely egalitarian Berber ancestors, the haughty Tuareg have a five-level caste system. The noble *Imochar*, experts in warfare, collect tribute from the camel-herding *Imrad* vassals;

22. The hut of the Ngwame Bantu – related both to the Swazi and the Zulu of South Africa – is a masterpiece of woven grass. The building of the framework is done by the men; it is then covered with mats woven by the women from several types of grass, providing superb insulation against temperatures varying regularly between 35°C and −4°C.

23. *(Right)* A village of pile-dwellings on Lake Nokwé in Benin, West Africa. Apart from fishing from canoes, the lake-dwellers practise an ingenious form of fish farming using *akadja*, submerged pens made from branches, which allow fish to spawn in great numbers. Work and residence are here very closely integrated.

agricultural work, which the nobles despise, is done by negro serfs, *Bella*; below them is a former slave group, *Iklan*, and an out-caste group, *Inaden*, the smiths and leatherworkers. Interestingly, this last group does not lead the nomadic life of the others, but lives in settled hamlets and travels out to service the dispersed Tuareg camps.

It might be thought that, under these most critical climatic conditions, house forms would be at their most rigidly determined, yet Tuareg dwellings take many forms. The sedentary agricul-turalists may live in square or rectangular houses built of mud or stone, beehive or barrel-vaulted huts, or even semi-subterranean houses. The nomads much prefer living in tents (they have a belief that they will contract an illness if they stay too long in a house) – either the mat-covered tents of the southern Tuareg or the more widespread skin tent (plate 25). On strictly practical grounds, the skin tent is often uncomfortable – it is not good at reflecting heat – but the Tuareg defend its use on aesthetic principles, and although often they will live in mat tents during the long dry spells, they switch to a skin tent as soon as cooling rains allow them to. Special care is taken when the women prepare a tent-cover for a newly married couple (amongst the northern Tuareg, the wedding ceremony itself is called *éhen*, which also translates as 'a tent'). After being tanned, the skins, usually from Barbary sheep, are treated with butter and red ochre, which makes them waterproof and gives them a deep red hue.

Other Berber desert-dwellers use tents made from woven strips of black goat-hair or camel-hair wool. A much more radical solution to the problem of the desert sun is found among the troglodyte Arabs from the Matmata Mountains of Tunisia, as also amongst the Siwans of Egypt, who use to advantage the almost infinite capacity of the earth to absorb heat by building under-ground. The typical sunken Matmata house has a large courtyard (about 30 feet square) from which lead six or more underground rooms, according to needs. Access is by means of a sloping tunnel to the courtyard, which is also the source of light and air.

To the south of the Sahara lies a belt of savannah country able to support cattle-herders such as the Fulani, who since the eleventh century have spread eastwards from their probable origin in Senegal, in a diaspora which today extends as far as Chad, two thousand miles away. It is therefore not surprising that they are known by many names – Fulani, Fellata, Fulbe, Peul and so on – since they are citizens of thirteen states, and their way of life is often intertwined with that of their many neighbours. Among the West African groups, the life of cattle-herding tends to preclude

24. An aerial view of the oasis town of El Oued in the Souf Region of the Algerian Sahara. The domed houses, made from gypsum plaster leached from the sand by underground water systems, are constructed using a rod to describe the radius of the horizontal courses of plaster bricks. The modular pattern of the courtyard houses with their domed rooms, preventing build-up of wind-blown sand, is a delight to the eye.

25. A goatskin tent of the Tuareg of extreme northern Upper Volta. The sides of the tent do not reach the ground, which facilitates the circulation of air.

attempts at agriculture; crops, once planted, would have to be abandoned, unless, as with some Fulani, the whole agricultural operation is handed over to serfs. Nomadism (or transhumance) is not the aimless wandering it may appear; the pastoralists are in fact slaves to their cattle, and must continually judge when and where to move their herds in order not to exhaust the mean pasture available.

Fulani houses vary with the type of nomadism which the group has adopted. Pure nomads have very simple shelters (plate 26) built with saplings bent in arcs over which woven mats are placed. When the group moves on, these mats are rolled up and taken on donkey-back, leaving the skeleton of saplings planted in the ground; if they can be re-used, so much the better. Yet even these very temporary encampments are not laid out in a haphazard way: certain groups use the east-west and north-south axes to express their notion of seniority. Each son of the chief is considered to be the head of his own lineage; the most senior son and his lineage camp furthest to the west, the youngest son to the east. Within

26. A typical nomadic Fulani (Fulbe) dwelling, east of Dori in northern Upper Volta. Tightly woven fibre mats are strapped to a curved frame of strong branches, except where 'patches' of millet stalks have been added. The entrance to the hut faces southwest, away from the direction of the anticipated rainy season storms.

each lineage, the most senior families are to be found on the south, the most junior to the north, so that in terms of both genealogy (relationship to the chief) and age, each family knows its place.

More settled Fulani live in more earth-bound dwellings (plate 28). The walls will usually be either mud or woven millet straw, and the roofs made from bundles of grass; the doorway may be given emphasis with braided work. Other Fulani live as merchants in more substantial mud-built homes (as, for instance, aristocratic groups in Hausa cities, see below), but these groups are considered by the pastoralists to be 'drop-outs' from the Fulani way of life.

South of Timbuctu and the Sahara, in the bend of the Niger River in Mali, is a geological scar of sandstone 125 miles long known as the Bandiagara escarpment. These cliffs are 1,000 feet high in places, and have provided a cordon against the incursions of Islam for the inhabitants, who are known to the surrounding Muslims as the Habbe ('unbelievers'). The unbelievers, in fact, have a richness and originality of symbolic and religious thought that makes them unique even in Africa. This is the land of the Dogon, whose way of life and thought has been revealed in the masterful fieldwork of Marcel Griaule, Germaine Dieterlen and their colleagues.

The Dogon are famed for their dramatic sculpture and masks, which for them possess strong magical powers, and are called by them the *Tellem*. This is also the name given to the people who once

27. *(Above left)* An aerial view of Logone-Birni in the Cameroun, with its abundance of screened spaces; the fluidity of movement between the closed and open structures draws the whole of the settlement into the domestic space.

28. *(Above)* The Fulani village of Fetombaga, southwest of Dori in northern Upper Volta. The Fulani here are farmers, not pastoralists, and live in thatched houses with walls of mud-brick. The trees were planted by the villagers to give shade.

29. The beetle-like mat tents of the Songhai, from the Niger bend near Timbuctu, Mali. Even in this settled community, the tents are retained as a link with a less sedentary past; they are also more comfortable on hot nights for sleeping, and as extra rooms for guests. A very different form of village for the same people is illustrated in plate 13.

lived in the cliffs, and who fled when the Dogon settled. So alive is the event in the minds of the Dogon that the Tellem are still considered to have title to the land that the Dogon have worked since sometime in the tenth to the fourteenth centuries.

The Dogon are oppressed by drought (it is one of the few places in Africa where the genuine visitor is not immediately welcomed with food), and the harsh sun continuously dries the loose sandy soil and scrub. Only in June is a brief and heavy rainfall expected, and this allows the Dogon to nurse their fields of onions and millet, laid out spirally (for this is how they conceive of their world's creation) in the form of a net, with tiny walls to retain the water. The Dogon are builders of four main types of structure: *ginna* or 'great houses', dwellings of two storeys, square granaries capped with grass cone roofs, and *toguna* or men's meeting-houses. The villages, sited on the cliff plateau, on the plain below, or, most spectacularly, merging with the cliff debris itself, are laid out according to a cosmological scheme. Not all the members of the community would be able to give an explicit account of this cosmology – this knowledge is the special property of the senior men – but it is true to say that all the villagers are profoundly conscious of its presence in their lives and it has a powerful influence on the shape of their living space.

In Griaule's book *Conversations with Ogotemmêli*, one wise elder has given an explanation of the ideal village layout. The fact

30. A view from the cliffs of Sanga, a village of the Dogon in the high plains near Banani.

31. A cliff debris village of the Dogon from the Bandiagara escarpment in Mali, photographed about 1950. The courtyard houses and straw-capped granaries are laid out in a complex scheme of sexual and reproductive anthropomorphism, heavily constrained by the stone terraces and the cliff itself. Beyond lies the Sahara Desert.

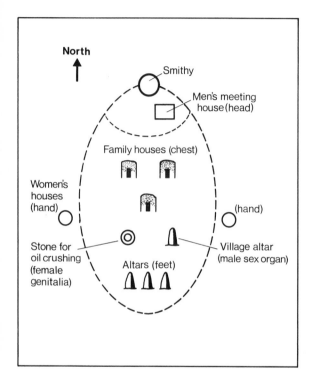

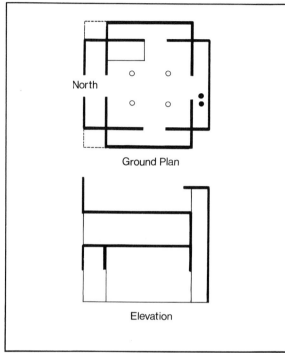

that the universe is projected in the same manner on a series of different scales – the cosmos, the village, the house, the individual – provides a profoundly unifying element in Dogon life. At the level of the village, the settlement should lie north to south, like a man on his back. The smithy and the council-house (*toguna*) are the man's head – where decisions are taken. The hands are symbolized by menstrual lodges on the east and west which are round, like wombs. The patriarchal *ginna* houses are the chest and belly; the oil-crushing stones and foundation altar represent the female and male sexual parts respectively, and are supposed to be located in the centre of the village. (In practice, the phallic altar is usually placed outside the walls, to show the correct attitude of modesty and respect towards women.) At the south of the village are the communal altars, the reclining man's feet.

The tiny houses (in which it is generally necessary to crouch or stoop) are enclosed quadrangles of adobe, two storeys high (Fig. 4). The internal square is the main room, in which the couple sleeps and the woman works, spinning and weaving narrow widths of cloth. Off each side of this room are adjoining rectangular store-rooms. The north-facing entrance vestibule represents the male, with the outer door being his sexual organ. The room opposite the

Fig. 3. (*Above left*) The idealized layout of a Dogon village, Mali. Like the house (Fig. 4), the village is laid out according to a consistently anthropomorphic scheme. (*after M. Griaule*)

Fig. 4. (*Above*) The two-storey Dogon house, in elevation and plan. (*after M. Griaule*)

32. *(Above)* A *togu na* ('house of speech') of the Dogon in the Kokoro quarter at Banani, a cliff-debris village below the Niger bend in Mali. This building was constructed in 1975 to replace its predecessor, one of the most ancient on the rocky escarpment, and manages to retain the former building's extraordinary visual impact.

33. *(Above right)* Entrance to the *togu na*, with a profusion of creatures in bas-relief: spotted crocodile, decorated hyena and leopard, and the characteristic *kanaga* masked figures. The serpent-like mythological *Nommo* represent life-giving moisture and the greenness to come.

entrance is the kitchen and hearth. The female genitals are symbolized by the door between the entrance and the central room, the woman's domain. The ground floor of the house is regarded as the woman lying on her back, ready for sexual intercourse. The man is thought of as the ceiling, his skeleton the beams, the four posts the couple's arms. Their breath rises from where their heads are, the hearth room, which is open to the heavens. A woman in childbirth undergoes labour in the central room, facing away from the entrance and supported by other women. Thus the child collects its life spirit, *nyama*, in the place where it was conceived. This close identification of the individual with the house continues even after death. The *nyama* leaves the body at the moment of death, and would roam like an 'uncovenanted spirit' (to borrow a term from theology), causing illness and damage to the village, if not prevented by being given a funeral rite, and encouraged to lodge in a statue; once collected, the ancestor spirit joins the other ancestors in a sanctuary in the great house of the lineage, the *ginna*.

An indispensable part of village architecture is the men's shelter, or *toguna*. Here the elders sit in the shade of the massive thatch (plates 32, 38) and elaborately greet whoever passes by.

34. The distinctive low dwellings of the Maasai, from
Ngorongoro, Tanzania. These people have villages for the
elders and their families, and also villages for the warrior age-
grades, known as *manyattas*. In the latter case the huts are
arranged in a circle with a cattle kraal in the centre. The
streamlined profile of the dwellings has advantages in the
high windy plateaux of Tanzania and Kenya. The stockade in
the rear of this photograph is a cattle-pen.

35. A Hutu hut from Rwanda. For five hundred years until
the mid-twentieth century the Hutu, along with the Twa,
were agriculturalist vassals to the pastoralist Tutsi,
and built houses for them as part of their service. The
circular mud house with conical thatch roof is the commonest
in the whole of Africa.

Occasionally they come to decisions on important matters, but mostly they chat, rest and take shade from the African sun. In ideal terms, this 'house of speech' is supported by eight great pillars of wood, aligned in a north-south direction (the outer six in three rows of two). The pillars are numbered anti-clockwise, with pillars 7 and 8 in the middle, forming a double quincunx. Numbers have a concrete significance to the Dogon, and in this case the eight numbered pillars represent the eight prime ancestors; *Nommo*, the primeval snake, is thought to twine around the outer six pillars, marking out the seventh ancestor (the master of speech) and the eighth (the Word itself).

The thoroughgoing anthropomorphism of the Dogon, which has only been touched on here, may strike the reader as perhaps an attempt to interpret too fancifully what may be simply convenient geographical metaphors. The gap between the ideal layout and the reality as delineated by tape-measure and compass may seem extraordinarily large at times. For example, the *toguna* pictured in plate 38 clearly diverges from the description given above; similarly, the village layout which can be seen in plate 30 is so constrained by the terrain that it can show few of the features of the ideal pattern. But this should not cause us to reject the Dogon's explanations. The riddle of outward appearances, considered as a veil through which immutable truth can be sporadically glimpsed and perpetually reinterpreted, has been grappled with in western thought since Plato. The Dogon's explanation of their spatial ideal offers a key to an understanding of the very different outlook of these tribesmen.

Other tribes from the western Sudan only marginally affected by Islam, such as the six Voltaic groups described by Prussin (1969), have settlements which vary from the roundhouse prototype of former times. Prussin suggests that the acceptance or rejection of externally imposed forms (as, for example, the flat-roofed rectangular or courtyard house originating from the north, its advantages for defence favouring its adoption) tells us much about the cultural history, the contacts and the dynamism of these communities. In certain more isolated parts of West Africa, this defensive style of housing has been taken much further. The Somba from the Atakora massif of northern Benin, for example, whom successive central authorities have found difficult to administer because of their proud individualism, are proper castle-dwellers (the Ssola of Togo and the Tambernu of Upper Volta are others). Their two- or even three-storey round towers of puddled mud (a material of great strength, which allows even taller structures, such as the Yemeni houses illustrated in plate

36. (*Above*) The Sherbro, from Shenge on the coast of Sierra Leone, build their large hipped-roof houses using horizontal laths tied to specially cultivated saplings with stringy bark. A week or so after the first application of mud, the second lot is applied, heavily keyed to take the final application of clay for the smooth finish. Specially favoured is white clay, which is also used for body decoration. The wooden framework is merely a form of 'internal scaffolding' as in this tropical forest region termites will completely remove it once the house is established.

38. The south side of a *togu na* from Madougou, a Dogon village on the plain, Mali. This meeting-house is characterized by its departure from the normal pattern of alignment of the pillars. The access is guarded by two female figures on posts facing each other. The heavy insulating thatch is of millet straw (compare this with plate 32).

37. *(Left)* More the work of a potter than a builder, the extraordinary thin-walled mud domes of the Mousgoum from northern Cameroun are built without any framework or supports. The embossed outer shell helps to shed rain and is also strikingly decorative.

18) are set in a circle, with a two-storey curtain wall linking them, which creates a yard on the inside and a forbidding rampart outside. The yard is partly roofed over with hardened clay supported on forked posts, forming a solid terrace where much of the domestic life is carried on. Sexes are strongly demarcated, and part of the motivation for this type of castle is probably to protect and regulate the women of the compound. Women spend much of their time on the roof terrace, where they can greet and comment on passers-by who can be seen coming from a good distance away; the women even sleep on the roof, in tiny low sleeping-huts with near-impassable entrances. The compound's single ground-floor exit is controlled by the senior male.

A very distinctive house-form commonly found in East Africa is the loaf-shaped hut of the Maasai, cattle pastoralists who migrate from rift valley to high plateau to escape summer drought. Their territory inconveniently extends over parts of both Kenya and Tanzania, and is defended by *morani*, conscripted warriors with a reputation for fierceness and photogeneity. The Maasai have two types of village: the first, the *manyatta*, or warrior kraal, is, intriguingly, built for the young men by their mothers, and the junior warriors are allowed to take young girls to their 'bachelor huts' to sleep. The *morani* must, however, become senior warriors and pass out as junior elders before they can marry and establish their own family kraal, the second sort of village. A typical household kraal will consist of an elder and three or four wives and their married sons, comprising perhaps thirty or so of the unusual low elliptical huts with their off-centre doorways (plate 34). The huts belong to the women, who are solely responsible

39. A village of the Orma Galla of Kenya. The simple cupola of grass thatch, while insubstantial, may be repaired or replaced with little effort.

40. A Labwor (Acholi) *ot* or round-hut from Uganda. Apart from a slightly raised sleeping bench, the house is undivided inside. The roof is supported not by the walls, but by posts, and the resulting verandah provides some shade.

for their construction and repair (an almost daily necessity when the rainfall is heavy; the technique is simply to smear fresh cow-dung on the roofs). The framework is made from interlacing pliant stakes over a ridge pole, and this forms a resilient vaulted ceiling strong enough to support the repairers. Just inside the door is an area where calves are sheltered at night and stores are kept. At the far end behind a partition are the beds, the wife's on the left of her husband's which is kept ready, even if he should only visit for a few days in as many weeks. In the middle is an 'entertaining' area, which even during the heat of the day has a fire burning; this provides light – and unwanted heat – around which women may sit and chatter, while drinking tea to cool themselves.

It would be misleading to give the impression that most Africans live in dispersed settlements or are constantly on the move with their portable dwellings. The contemporary African is powerfully drawn to the advantages, not unmixed with drawbacks, of life in

42. A house in Djenne, Mali. Like Timbuctu 250 miles to the north, Djenne was an important trading centre for gold and salt on the trans-Saharan route, with a large merchant class amassing great wealth. The typical Djenne merchant's house has sweeping vertical buttresses moulded from mud plaster mixed with vegetable oil.

41. A wall surrounding a Hausa compound in northern Nigeria, built, like the houses, from pear-shaped mud-bricks and plastered over. Privacy and the seclusion of women are important to the Hausa, who are Muslims. They have a proverb: 'Aeroplanes are the remedy for the jealous husband'.

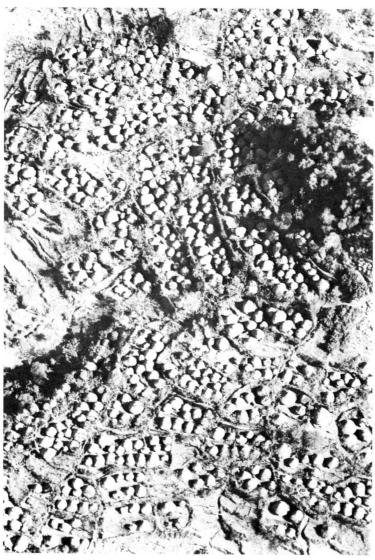

43. *(Left)* The town of Buso, a compact settlement of the Konso from south-western Ethiopia. The farming households, remarkable for their high densities, form quarters on the basis of clan and ritual groupings; each quarter has its men's houses where, through abstinence, sexual energy is believed to be transformed into power for hunting and warfare.

44. *(Right)* A Hausa house from Kano, northern Nigeria, sculptured in non-representational bas-relief. The *zanko* or 'rabbit's ears' at roof level have been interpreted as swords or phallic symbols, but there is no agreement on the true explanation of this characteristic feature of Hausa building (they are also to be seen on the Hausa wall, plate 41).

the modern city, although his migration is often no more than seasonal or a means of finding a job while tenaciously maintaining his links with the homestead. But apart from such newly developing cities there are many towns with a very high population density, such as Buso in Ethiopia (plate 43), and of great antiquity. Ancient monuments are rare in much of Africa owing to the scanty distribution of stone, one of the few materials to withstand the ravages of climate, and this rarity makes them all the more spectacular. At Koumbi-Saleh (possibly the capital of ancient

45. A 'modern' Hausa house, also from Kano. Polychrome painting has been used to exaggerate the arabesques of the mud façades. A roof of *bati*, or tin, has great prestige in parts of Africa, where it is rapidly replacing thatch. The tin roof is hot in the summer, cold in the winter and very noisy during rain, but requires less maintenance.

Ghana) remains of a medieval commercial centre survive. In Rhodesia, Zimbabwe, the 'stone house', comprising various buildings enclosed in an elliptical wall of granite blocks, was probably the seat of the divine kingdom of Monomotapa, the 'Lord of the Mines', and dates from as early as the fifth century. In the hills of Tanzania at Engaruku are the remarkable remains of what was once a town of six thousand flat-roofed houses, with tombs, terraces and stone circles; it is a relic of the Azanian agricultural civilization, and dates from the eighth century.

Other settlements of antiquity, such as the terminal posts of the trade route across the Sahara – Walata, Djenne, Timbuctu, Gao and Kano – all became wealthy and important centres after the conquest of the northern coast by Islam by the eighth century. Originally developed as an exchange of salt from the north for gold from the south, the trade was extended to include ivory, slaves, leather, dyed fabrics and other products. Wherever man trades, he exchanges more than goods, and in this case the most significant

46. The house of Nyimi, chief of the Bushongo Kuba from Mushenge, Kasai, central Zaire, photographed in 1928. Finely wrought decorative mats, made from split palms tied to reeds, were attached to the framework; matting fences surrounded the compounds.

product was the promulgation of the Islamic faith itself.

The Arab traders were to have a profound effect on native building styles, not only because of the centrifugal forces of commerce, but through their wealthy families' need for secure dwellings, and their insistence on the seclusion of women. *The Holy Qur'ān* speaks of the requirement for wives of the prophet to 'stay in your house and display not your beauty like the displaying of the ignorance of yore' (Sūra 22, verse 33). The effect is clearly seen in the mud cities of the Hausa from northern Nigeria. The principal cities of Kano, Kakawa, Sokoto and Zaria, also at the ends of trade routes, formed focii for the cluster of small states known as Hausaland, which swept to importance in the fifteenth century (although some of the cities had been founded four hundred years earlier). Hausaland owed its integrity to its political sophistication, its language – influenced by Arabic and written in Arabic script – and the adoption of Islam. The distinctive compound houses are built with red laterite soil rich in clay and are clustered around the central palace, mosque and market; narrow winding footpaths thread their way between the walls, which in the larger compounds are forbiddingly high. The walls are constructed first (plate 41): the buildings inside are tailored to meet the changing needs of a family structure where divorce and adoption are frequent as well as natural increase. Established compounds have a single entrance hut (*zaure*) through which few non-family males will be allowed; even they will not pass beyond the *shigifa*, the inner entrance, through which only husbands are allowed. The wives' reputations could not be better guarded! But Hausa architecture is better known for the elaborately sculptured mud façades (plate 44). Usually only the entrance doorway and its surrounding wall is decorated, but sometimes prosperous men like to draw attention to their building, and commission a decorator to cover the whole surface, even the interior (though this will not be seen by strangers or visitors), with bas-relief arabesques and contrasting colours. Islamic art is non-representational, but the pragmatic Hausa accommodate recognizable artifacts – guns, swords, bicycles and so on – in their bold motifs, and the effect is vivid and powerful.

47. Houses of the Manga of Zaire, showing the framework of a house under construction. These unusual forms were also built by the Ngelima, Panga and Nalya, all from Zaire, but the particular village layout varied.

The Americas

48. (*Left*) A man of the Barasana Indians of Colombia decorating the front end of a *basi wa*, a longhouse which is also used as a ceremonial centre and dance-house. The symbolic paintings on the end walls add to the prestige already gained by the hosts in building the house.

The North American continent was populated over 27,000 years ago by Palaeo-Indians, who crossed from Siberia by a land bridge and slowly dispersed, helped by an ice-free corridor into central North America. The pedestrian explorers, following herds of bison and caribou from the Pacific fringes of Siberia, reached Tlapacoya in Mexico 23,000 years ago, and had drifted further to the highlands of South America 3,000 years after this. Evidence for waves of overland migration along what is today known as the Bering Strait is revealed not only by recent archaeological discoveries but also by linguistic affinities between New World languages and Palaeo-Siberian. In more recent times Pre-Columbian contacts definitely occurred, but were too slight to have had a significant effect on the population of the continent.

North American aboriginal cultures are sometimes divided into three main groups: Aleuts (western Eskimos from the Aleutian Islands), Inuit (Eskimos from North Alaska, Canada and Greenland who all speak dialects of Inukpik), and Indians. The three groups represent successive pulses in the migration from Asia, though the Indians cannot be considered as homogeneous since they embrace a tremendous variety of peoples. At the time of European contact, more than 400 distinctive cultures existed altogether, although we have reliable knowledge of many fewer.

The stereotyped view that Eskimos live in igloos and Indians live in tepees masks the real diversity of aboriginal houses. In the Inuit area alone, the efforts to overcome the twin problems of the

49. A hemispherical mat tent of the wild-rice-gathering Ojibwa from Canada. Village life existed only in the summer for these people, when three to fifteen families came together; by the winter, these families dispersed to take maximum advantage of game resources. As with many hunter-gathering bands, villages were not stable in number or location for any length of time.

50. An igloo from Lindstrom valley, photographed by Raul Amundsen, showing the radial arrangement of rooms off the central chamber.

ferociously cold climate and the paucity of the more usual building materials have brought forward very individual solutions. In the west, excavated earth lodges on a rectangular plan are widespread, but the roof style varies: it may be round, hipped (i.e. with four slopes), or flat and made from bark (as with the Chugach of Alaska). Hunting peoples commonly lived in conical or cupola tents of hide in the brief summer, but retreated to more permanent dwellings with stone walls and earth roofs for the winter. Even true igloo builders, such as the Caribou Inuit, also used simple conical tents, and two of the most northerly-living tribal peoples in the world, the Tareumiut of Point Barrow and the Polar Eskimo of Greenland, did not build igloos at all, but semi-subterranean domes of sod in the one case and stones in the other. The excavated lodge is also characteristic of the peoples of tribal Siberia, which suggests that the migrants may have brought the idea with them.

Despite its less than universal adoption by the Inuit, it is nevertheless understandable that the igloo (plate 50) is so familiar as an idea to the westerner, for its beautiful simplicity transcends the limitations of climate and material. The dome encloses the greatest volume for the smallest surface area of any wide-based structure, so heat losses through wind-chill are minimized. The igloo is made

51. Earth lodges of the Californian Indians in the Sacramento valley. The doorway, which was sometimes at ground level, is in this case directly on top of the house (as with the adobe house of the Pueblo Indians of New Mexico). Other earth lodges in this area included the L-shaped type of the Gallinomero, with a heavy thatched roof, and the conical or wedge-shaped type of the Yokut, arranged in a row with a single awning of brushwood running its length, providing shade in front.

52. (*Overleaf*) A settlement on the Georgian Bay area of Lake Huron, probably of Ottawa Indians, painted in about 1845 by Paul Kane (1810–71). Both the wigwams and the canoes are made from birch-bark.

from a single material – snow which has not become too dense through settling – cut into rectangular blocks and laid not in horizontal courses, but spirally. This means that the structure is self-supporting throughout, the blocks being trimmed to slope inwards until the key-block is added from outside. The builder then makes an exit, adding a tunnel of snow blocks which is below the level of the living quarters in order to drain cold air away by convection. A sleeping platform, raised on a block of packed snow above the cold-air level, occupies the rear of the chamber. If the house is to be more than an overnight hunting shelter, then vented cooking rooms and storage chambers are added as needed, radially linked to the main room by tunnels. A window of ice is sometimes inserted in the wall as a finishing touch.

From the wide variety of Indian cultures, we can distinguish three major types of building, in addition to the familiar tepee; these are the gable-roofed wooden houses, the earth lodges and the tiered adobe village houses named by the Spanish 'pueblos'. The first of these, hewn from giant red cedars which soar 200 feet high with barely a knot, are characteristic of the Northwest coast tribes from southern Alaska and British Columbia. These tribes (the Kwakiutl, Haida, Tlingit and Bellacoola are the best known) are

organized into lineages considered to be the descendants of a particular animal 'ancestor'; each lineage occupies one of the vast communal longhouses built along the lower reaches of rivers. The plank houses (a Tlingit example is shown in plate 53) – like the huge totem poles which attest to the pride of the lineage in its ancestral demi-gods – are surely an example of material suggesting form. Although carpentry was accomplished (at least in the pre-contact period) without the benefit of steel tools – adzes were made with stone blades, chisels with bone, and shells were used as finishing scrapers – these people were nevertheless highly skilled, as is demonstrated by the craftsmanship of their decorated storage chests. These were made from a single board, scored and bent at the corners by steaming, and fixed to the base by stitching. The decoration of these boxes, as on their blankets, totem poles and house panels, is in a distinctive flat style. The design is generally an animal, split down either the spine or the belly, and spreadeagled; so stylized is the representation that the animal is often unidentifiable to all but a few. This obscurity is often intensified by the artist's indulging in visual puns, as well as the general exuberance of the design.

The climate of the Northwest coast is much milder than the latitude might suggest because of warm ocean currents. In fact, this area overflows with natural abundance; apart from the wealth of food in the forests, salmon in their thousands could be caught during the season. The houses themselves were constructed of curved overlapping boards fixed to six or eight massive cedar pillars. In the busy spring hunting and fishing seasons, the external cladding of the houses was sometimes removed and taken to temporary settlements where it was attached to other frames – which shows that not all portable structures need be light and fragile. Inside, a raised sleeping platform extended round the inner walls, with mat screens to divide the dozen or so families which shared the lineage's house. The noblest families customarily occupied the section furthest from the door, thus enjoying the greatest comfort and safety. The growth of material benefits often has a tendency to deflect a society's attention from spiritual pre-occupations; yet here the affluence, though extravagantly displayed, was also channelled into sacred ritual. The winter season, when vast stockpiles of food had been accumulated, saw the transformation of the dwelling houses into great sacred theatres, the scene of cycles of drama and initiation ordeals.

In contrast to the northwest, with its mild maritime climate and lush forests, are the Great Plains. This vast area, bounded in the west by the Rockies and in the east by great stretches of forest, is a

53. *(Left)* A chief's house of the Tlingit, in Cape Fox, Alaska. Among the Tlingit a boy leaves his home at around the age of eight or ten to live under the guidance of his maternal uncle; this avunculocal residence gives the father of the boy more authority than would full matrilocal residence. The painting and totem-pole proclaim that the house belongs to the bear clan.

55. *(Right)* Earth lodges of the Mandan Indians of the mid-western USA. The houses were about forty feet in diameter, with a central smoke-hole (which also admitted light) about four feet in diameter; in heavy rain upturned boats were used to cover the hole.

treeless belt that varies from grassland to near-desert. The Plains Indians – Ojibwa, Blackfoot, Cree in the north, Crow, Hidatsa, Dakota, Cheyenne in the centre, and Kiowa, Comanche, Apache in the south – include the feather-headdressed equestrian warriors of popular imagination, the 'typical Indian'. In fact this stereotype Indian culture existed for a comparatively brief interlude only, from the acquisition of horses brought over by the Spaniards to the extinction of the American Bison (the correct name for the 'buffalo') two and a half centuries later. Before then, the Plains Indian lived a settled existence in much the same way as his eastern neighbours, planting squash and maize and hunting the occasional deer or stray buffalo; dog travois (A-frame sleds) were used for transport. The arrival of the horse brought an ecological revolution: the massive herds of buffalo could now be hunted on a large scale. The cycle of nomadism was closely adapted to that of the buffalo, which gathered in their thousands in the late summer mating season and dispersed into smaller herds in winter and spring. The Indians too would come together for communal hunting in late summer, when ceremonial activity reached its peak, then break into kindred groups or small bands for the rest of the year.

While they were horticulturalists these Indians lived mainly in earth lodges; the Mandan (plate 55), Arikara, Hidatsa and Pawnee (plate 54) retained them, at least for ceremonial use, even after their way of life altered and they became buffalo hunters.

54. *(Left)* A rare photograph of the interior of an earth lodge of the Pawnee, Plains Indians of the Mid-West. Note the central fire-pit and raised sleeping-platform around the edge; light is provided by the central smoke-hole in the roof.

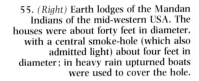

Their rype corne

Their greene corne

Corne newly sprong

Their sitting at meate

The place of solemne prayer

The house wherin the Tombe of their Herounds standeth.

SECOTON·

A Ceremony in their prayers w[ith] strange iestures and songes dansing abowt posts carued on the topps lyke mens faces.

56. The village of Secotan in Virginia (now included in North Carolina), by John Wyth (White). The painting was made on Sir Richard Grenville's expedition in 1585, and shows scattered wigwams amid fields of tobacco, corn and melons. (The English word 'wigwam' is from the Ojibwa generic term for 'house', cognate with the Menomini term *wēkewam*). The small hemispherical structure in the top right-hand corner of the picture is a raised sentry-box.

57. The 'Cliff Palace' in the Mesa Verde National Park in Colorado. The brick building dates from the Pueblo III Culture of about AD 1100–1300, although the caves themselves show evidence of occupancy dating back to 10,000 BC. There are several hundred cliff and pueblo dwellings in the Mesa Verde.

These large earth houses (usually 40 feet or more in diameter) were partitioned internally with buffalo skins or willow matting, the compartments giving onto a central communal area with its fire-pit. The tepee (the name comes from the Dakota word for 'dwelling'), on the other hand, being easily erected and dismantled, was ideally suited to tracking the unpredictable buffalo herds. The structure of the conical tent (plate 58) varied little over the whole of the Great Plains area; it was composed of twenty or so soft buffalo hides stretched over a frame. The cover was the wife's property, being given to her by her family on marriage, and represented a good deal of labour value; this matrilineal mode of inheritance was quite possibly a link with the horticultural past, when women played a dominant role in the extensive farming activity. Four main poles of pine, precious because they were carried great distances from the eastern woodlands, were lashed together at the top to form the frame. Two flaps at the top of the cover, adjusted by means of longer poles, ingeniously controlled ventilation, allowing smoke to escape without letting in draughts. Inside, an antechamber was formed by a hide curtain, behind which the owner and her husband slept on the left, with children and dependants on the right. As well as hide, bark was commonly used to cover the tepee – several tribes from the Great Lakes area, as well as the Ottawa Algonkians (plate 52), used bark, whilst the Dakota and Montagnais had tents made from both bark and hide.

Bark homes of a quite different type – called longhouses – were used by the Iroquois of New York State. The League of the Iroquois, a sophisticated confederacy of 'Five Nations' – the Mohawk, Oneida, Onondaga, Cayuga and Seneca – held cultural leadership over all the Indians of the northeast at the time of European contact. They were organized into matrilineal clans (i.e. membership being through the mother), the sons bringing home their wives, and on occasion daughters their husbands, to the maternal establishment. The longhouse was a symbol of identity to the Iroquois (they called themselves *Hodénosaunee* – 'people of the longhouse'), and it was built on a rectangular plan to a great variety of lengths. It could be extended indefinitely to house additions to the clan, which consisted of from four to twenty or more families, each living in a small apartment on either side of a central corridor. These cubicles were rather small – only about six feet wide – and were heated by a fire in the corridor for every four units; sleeping platforms were constructed at the rear of each one and the space between the roof poles and the arched roof of elm-bark shingles was used for storing supplies. Iroquois settlements looked much like the charming painting of the Powhatan Indian

58. A decorated tepee of the Blackfoot Indians from Montana. The Blackfoot are the most northern of the Plains Indians, the culture group which alone used this distinctive portable dwelling of buffalo-hide.

village of Secotan by John Wyth (plate 56), although because of their larger-scale political integration, an Iroquois village might have as many as three thousand inhabitants, and would set up an elaborate defence system of palisades and a moat.

A comparable type of sedentary communal life existed among the Pueblo Indians of the southwest. The Pueblos (Spanish for both 'peasant villages' and 'people') of this region were so called by Francisco Coronado, who in 1540 travelled from Mexico City in search of the seven fabled cities of Cibola – the cities of gold. He found no gold, but instead the adobe (mud-brick) houses of the Zuñi, piled on top of each other for three, four or five storeys. Although the villages are widely separated because of the scattered water supplies, the houses are clumped together in the otherwise empty landscape. This arrangement helps to shape the religious and social organization of these Indians, which has proved resilient to the many outside forces of change. Today, as before, the stress is still on equality and co-operation with a careful respect for the environment; there is no attempt to make rooms larger or more ostentatious than those built hundreds of years before, which might suggest that concerns of prestige rather than 'basic needs' influence the building of larger forms. Access to each floor of the complex is still by ladders from the floor below, and the *kiva* or men's ceremonial house, sunk below ground level and entered from the roof, remains a distinctive feature. The northern part of this chamber, which is a council and workroom besides, is the location of the *sipapu* – a pit or depression in the floor symbolizing the sacred place of the emergence of all mankind from the various underworlds. The unpartitioned terraced rooftops are considered common space, as is the central 'plaza', used for dancing.

As far as architectural monumentality is concerned, none of the examples drawn upon in this book compares with the triumphs of the Aztec of Mexico, the Central American Maya of Guatemala, or the Inca of Peru, who built ceremonial structures on a quite breathtaking scale. The Peruvian fortress of Sacsahuamán outside Cuzco, for example, was made from giant stones – the largest weighed 360 tons – which had to be transported 40 miles over mountain paths to form triple ramparts; the masonry-work was so skilled that the point of a knife can barely be inserted between the keyed joints. Certainly, civilizations as complex as these, comparable to any of the contemporary high civilizations in the Old World, with a highly organized state, a division of labour and class, and the establishment of city life, cannot really be termed 'tribal'. The collapse of the political order and the overthrow of the dominant priesthood-intelligentsia was rapid enough to account for the

60. *(Right)* A house of a Mayan Indian, in the village of San Estevan, Belize, Central America. The photograph was taken during one of the tropical downpours which necessitate annual repairs to the thatched roof.

lack of influence of these extraordinary cultures in modern times. But in some areas such as Guatemala and Belize, the Mayan language and cultural identity is still predominant, and the humble Maya house (plate 60) shows a link with the ancestral dwelling.

The other, more specifically tribal societies of the South American continent still face the threat of acculturation, even extinction. The rich and complex local cultures of the Amazon Basin, for example, which have adapted themselves so sensitively to the rain-forest ecology, preserving the thin soil of the forest floor by swidden, or slash-and-burn cultivation, seem soon to be swept away in the tide of expansion into this area. Their brightest hope for the future seems to be in resettlements like the Xingú River reserve, but they are as likely to end up as subject cultures in today's frontier land.

The whole Amazon Basin is characterized by scattered communities of extended families living in large communal houses (commonly called *malocas*). The Panare of Venezuela, who live on several small tributaries of the middle Orinoco, are a typical example. Their territory is mixed: forested mountains are interspersed with broken plains with mainly savannah vegetation, the forests generally providing the richer resource. Their houses are conical in shape (plate 14), but there are even larger houses, often rectangular in floor-plan with a bay at each end, so that they resemble upturned ship's hulls. Their palm thatching rarely lasts

59. *(Left)* A village scene from Brazilian Amazonia, showing the important central 'plaza'.

61. *(Left)* A 'war gathering' of the Witoto Indians of southeastern Colombia, outside their communal house. The Witoto tribe is a linguistic rather than a political unit, being divided into autonomous and sometimes hostile clans, each owning a huge longhouse, oval in plan. The roof is made of palm leaves fastened to split bamboo, overlapping in layers a foot thick.

62. *(Left)* A *maloca* (communal longhouse) of the Barasana, undergoing decoration. The front of the house is very much associated with men and male activities, the apsidal rear end with women and female activities such as cooking; each sex has its own door at opposite ends.

63. *(Right)* A village dwelling of the Yagua, Marañón River, an Amazon tributary in Peru. The airy raised platform of split bamboo provides a good solution for coping with the damp tropical climate.

more than four rainy seasons, after which the inhabitants — a group of thirty to forty people, mostly extended family — will build a new house within a three-mile radius rather than repair the old one.

Throughout the dry season the Panare leave their communal *malocas* because they become too hot inside, lacking any form of cross-ventilation. Although this house design seems irrational in that climate, the Panare make up for it by the simple expedient of the hammock. As soon as the temperature and humidity become too much, they set up temporary camps wherever they hear that fish are plentiful, or there is some ripe wild fruit, in a part of the forest where they can fix their hammocks in the shade of trees. This simple device is, like the use of the highly effective blowpipe for hunting, a common feature of the tribes of the great forests. It solves several problems: it has a negligible heat capacity so heat does not build up, it lifts the sleeper above much of the teeming

insect life, and it is light, readily portable and quick to set up. Other tribes use this device inside their *malocas*; the internal arrangements vary from unpartitioned quarters for extended families, constituting a whole village, to societies in which nuclear families have separate apartments (such as the Witoto dwelling in plate 61).

There is frequently a strict division of labour between the sexes in these societies – men and women have their particular crops which they plant and harvest. Women generally have the time-consuming task of preparing cassava bread from the poisonous roots of the bitter manioc, while the men hunt and fish. These cultural divisions are often given concrete expression by sexual divisions about the *maloca*. Among the Barasana of the Vaupes region of Colombia, for example, the longhouse (plate 62) has a front door used by men and a rear door for women. The rear part of the house may be square or semi-circular, but in any case will be

screened off to form the female domain where cassava bread is prepared and children are attended to. Around the sides of the house towards the female end are stalls for each nuclear family. The front part of the house is associated with male activities: men often sit just inside the door during the day, talking and making baskets. Tobacco and coca leaves are prepared at the sides, but men will sit together at the centre of the house at night to smoke and chew coca. The central area may be used for communal meals during the daytime, but its most important use is for ritual and initiation dances, where a clearly marked path is provided by the eight major upright posts. Outside is the *maka*, an area meticulously cleared of weeds – neighbouring groups will ascribe prestige to the community on the basis of how well this is done. Surrounding the *maka* is an area of swidden, the *chagra*, which is considered the women's domain. From the *maka* the men's path leads to the forest and the river beyond; women leave by the rear door to their separate path from the clearing through the *chagra* to their washing-place and port on a stream leading to the river. A further case of

64. The simple dwellings of Tierra del Fuego, illustrated by Sydney Parkinson. Captain Cook wrote of them in January of 1769: 'Their Hutts are made like a behive (sic) and open on one side where they have their fire, they are made of small Sticks and cover'd with branches of trees, long grass &c in such manner that they are neither proff (sic) against wind Hail, rain or snow . . .'. *(quoted in Beaglehole)*

sexual division is the fact that, because of the custom of marrying-out, the Barasana women and men speak mutually unintelligible dialects, which they may retreat into using on specified occasions. Physical separation of the sexes is carried even further by the Mundurucu of Brazil, with all the men sleeping apart from their wives in a men's house.

Another type of communal dwelling, the open-walled hipped or gable-roofed house on piles, is erected by (among other peoples) the Yagua, who live on tributaries of the Peruvian Amazon. The problems of heat and humidity are overcome by building these raised airy platforms on a clearing by the river bank, to obtain the maximum benefit from the cooling breezes. The open-walled Yaguan structure (plate 63) houses a whole community, from which it might be expected that the lack of privacy would negate any climatic advantages in the design. But we have noted in the introduction to this book how the notion of 'privacy' is dependent on cultural attitudes, and in this case there is a specific and tacit social convention that anyone may 'absent' himself simply by turning away from the centre; anyone doing this – women and children share this privilege – will be neither looked upon nor disturbed (for several hours if required) so long as he faces the outside. Here, a cultural convention directly corresponds to the more familiar material convention of a partition to give privacy, a subtlety of which the archaeologist must perforce be unaware.

In contrast to the hot and humid climates of the tropical forest, the natives of Tierra del Fuego, the most southerly of all tribal peoples (they were driven to extinction at the end of the nineteenth century), lived in an inhospitable and stormy climate. The Ona, who lived inland on the island and hunted guanaco (a species of small wild camel), used a type of shelter that would be considered inadequate by most other societies. House building is not a universal phenomenon – there are many examples of tribes from Australia, Amazonia and Southeast Asia who never build – but such peoples at least enjoy comfortable temperatures. Not so the Ona, whose flimsy shelters were in the form of a dome cut in half (plate 64) on a semi-circular base, which left a 'doorway' wide open to the elements. Although the Ona had no art (in contrast to the Eskimo), they were not so technologically primitive that they could not build more elaborately, as is shown by the care with which their conical thatched huts, used only for ritual purposes, were fashioned. The Ona provide a most thought-provoking illustration of the argument that mankind responds primarily to cultural perceptions of his needs rather than immediate physical necessity.

Oceania

The Pacific Ocean is remarkable not only for its vastness but also for the tremendous number of islands scattered throughout – an estimated 25,000. Some are tiny atolls, accretions of coral only a few feet above sea-level; others are of volcanic origin and have mountains and precipitous cliffs, like the Hawaiian Islands and Tahiti, or they are of the continental type such as New Guinea and New Zealand – large islands with a variety of ecosystems.

The population of Oceania came from the west, along the island chains of Indonesia to the 1,300-mile-long island of New Guinea, the centre of the region named in the nineteenth century 'Melanesia' after its 'black-skinned' inhabitants (the other areas are Polynesia, the 'many islands', and Micronesia, the 'tiny islands'). A measure of cultural unity is given to Melanesia – which includes New Guinea, the Bismarck Archipelago (New Ireland and New Britain), the Solomon Islands, the New Hebrides and New Caledonia, as well as smaller islands – by the shared traits of yam and taro cultivation. Pigs are commonly domesticated also, sometimes to the extent that the animals are considered almost as members of the family, in a way reminiscent of East African herdsmen's religious devotion to their cattle. In contrast to Polynesia, where leaders are generally hereditary, leadership in Melanesia frequently goes to non-hereditary 'big-men', whose power derives from their skills in persuasive oratory and their virtuosity in handling the complex relationships built up over years by exchange of goods.

Villages are fairly small (except along the Sepik River in New Guinea where settlements may have a thousand inhabitants). Warfare used to be more or less continuous in Melanesia, and the villagers generally chose their site with defence in mind. Along the coast villages were set back from the shore out of sight, and in the highlands they would be built on mountain ridges, to allow for warning of attack from below (as with the Chimbu village of Gumine, plate 65). The natural fission of the population which led to this frequent warfare also resulted in the village being the largest political unit; although alliances were often made with neighbouring people, culturally and linguistically the village was usually highly autonomous.

Throughout Melanesia, it is common for an extended family to occupy its own house, though in the Gulf area of New Guinea large communal houses exist where a whole lineage shares a house. In the larger islands, houses are commonly built on piles. These have many advantages: on land, ground liable to flooding may be utilized, and the space beneath may be used for storage and allows a better circulation of air; over water, access by boat is easy and

HABITATIONS DU VILLAGE DE LIKILIKI.

(NOUVELLE – IRLANDE)

66. *(Above)* **An illustration from Duperrey's** *Voyage of the Coquille* **showing different types of building structures from Likiliki, New Ireland. Although this island is part of the Melanesian culture area, the raised stone-faced house platform is often considered a characteristically Polynesian feature.**

65. *(Left)* **Gumine, a village of the Chimbu in the eastern highlands of Papua-New Guinea, between the Waghi and Tua Rivers. The mountain ridge site provided valuable defence advantages in a region where warfare also accounts for the relative autonomy and the very localized styles and systems of political organization in the highland villages.**

some protection from insects is offered. Raised houses on either type of site have defence advantages. Apart from dwelling-houses proper, the impressive ceremonial or cult houses of men's societies are common throughout the area. Bachelors often sleep there, visitors are entertained, men lounge there to drink kava or chew betel nut and debate or gossip; but sacred objects are also prepared and displayed there, and complex initiation rituals are enacted. In the Solomon Islands, for example, the coastal people spend a great deal of time at sea fishing for bonito, and formerly used the celebrated *tomako* or war canoe, inlaid with nautilus shell. The canoe-houses on the shoreline, where the boys who were to become bonito fishermen were secluded before the rite, were therefore most magnificent buildings. Shrines set just inside the door, sculptures of sharks, frigate birds and sea-spirits in the shape of mermen, and other ritual apparatus necessary for the ceremonials to ensure success in fishing added to the mysterious gloom of the interior.

By far the most spectacular of Oceanic structures are the New Guinea men's houses known by the pidgin term *haus tambaran*. These cult houses are found all along the Sepik River, from its source in the central highlands to the lower Sepik region, as well as in the Maprik Mountains north of the river.

67. A beautifully woven court-house from Aola Bay, Guadalcanar, southeast Solomon Islands. This house type is thought to derive from New Georgia, where it was built by 'big men' or wealthy individuals only. The roof ridge and the wall plaiting are all typical of New Georgia; the rigorous symmetry is typical of much of Solomon Island art.

68. A village scene on Siar Island, Prince Heinrich Haven, New Guinea. The ingenious sloping gable-ends provide a shaded verandah to the houses; note the canoes stored under the raised floor, and the striking piece of sculpture outside the house on the left of the picture.

69. A bachelors' house in the fishing village of Tabadi, Humboldt Bay, Irian Jaya (West New Guinea). The tiered polygonal form shows some similarity to Indonesian structures to the west of New Guinea.

70. A women's house in the Chimbu
village of Dirima, eastern highlands of
Papua-New Guinea. The walls of the house
and the stockades are made from yar trees
(casuarina) which are cultivated for their
pig-proof qualities.

71. A dwelling-house over water from
Doreri in the Papuan Gulf, an illustration
from Duperrey's *Voyage of the Coquille*,
which lasted 32 months from 1821.
Compare this building with that in plate
72, a larger structure which shares some
stylistic features.

72. A vast *Ravi* (men's club-house) from
Kamari in the Purari Delta area of
Papua-New Guinea.

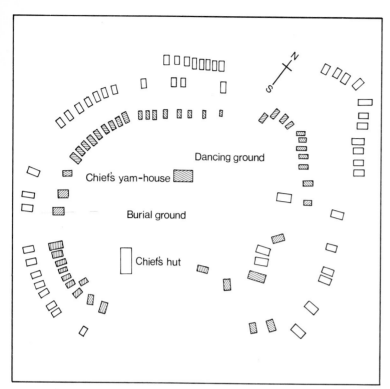

Dancing ground

Chief's yam-house

Burial ground

Chief's hut

Fig. 5. A plan of the village of Omarakana, Trobriand (Kiriwina) Islands, with its concentric layout. *(after B. Malinowski)*

The Abelam — a tribe of 30,000 in the foothills of the Prince Alexander Mountains of the Sepik District — have more than a hundred of these dramatic structures with triangular façades as high as 65 feet raked forward and dominating the *amei* (ceremonial ground) which forms the centre of the hamlet. The façades (plate 74) are mainly taken up with vigorous polychrome paintings of *nggwalndu*, stylized representations of clan spirits, also represented by painted sculptures inside the house, but who are considered to reside in reality in the huge carved figures secreted in the sanctum. The 'real' *nggwalndu* are only displayed to men at their final initiation — which can take two complete ceremonial cycles, or 20 to 30 years. The tambaran cult and its associated long-yam ritual are cults of male dominance, fertility (in an agricultural and sexual sense), and prestige — and the Abelam, tenacious practitioners of the tambaran cult, also happen to be one of the most 'progressive' tribes in terms of economic development. This is perhaps because the ritual is fulfilling and confirms their sense of identity, and also because the co-operation over long periods of time involved in 'passing out' effectively overcomes the aggressive individualism from which their neighbours suffer.

The yam also has great sociological significance in the eastern end of New Guinea, the Massim District, but the best-known account of the yam cult comes from Malinowski's classic account of the Trobriand (Kiriwina) Islands, near New Guinea's eastern tip. Malinowski stayed in the village of Omarakana, on the large flat coral island of Boyowa. The village plan is anything but haphazard; it is in the form of two concentric circles (see Fig. 5), the

73. A detail showing the junction of the house post and roof ridge poles of a men's ceremonial house from Kanganaman village, Middle Sepik River, Papua-New Guinea. The huge hardwood pillar is carved with a haunting stylized face representing a clan spirit. The exterior of this Iatmul house is illustrated on the front cover.

75. *(Above)* **The interior of a Sepik River meeting-house from Ambuti, Papua-New Guinea, showing the magnificently rich polychrome decoration to the roof.**

74. *(Left)* **A pyramidal** *haus tambaran* **at Kinbanggwa, north Abelam, Papua-New Guinea.** *Nggwalndu* **– clan spirits associated with masculinity, prestige and fertility – stare down from the brilliantly painted triangular façade of sago-spathe. Other representations of the same spirits, carved statues in a radically different style, are hidden from the uninitiated in the sanctum of the house.**

76. The chief's house, from Omarakana village in the Trobriand Islands. The chief, from the Tabalu sub-clan, being the highest-ranking in the islands, has the highest house. Every ornament is a sign of rank. The fish-birds on the gable boards are a combination of porpoises and kingfishers: the first is a purveyor of magical power, the second a bringer of fertility.

77. A seed yam-house belonging to the chief, also from Omarakana village. This is a closed, 'non-display' yam-house (*sokwaypa*) where the chief's unmarried sons occasionally sleep, quite different from the display yam-house (*bwayma*) illustrated in plate 80. The same decorative motifs recur.

outer 'profane' ring consisting of dwelling-houses (*lisiga*), the inner 'sacred' ring of elaborate yam-houses (*bwayma*). A street runs between the rows. The dwelling-houses of the chief's kin are rather plain and built on the ground, but the yam-houses are raised, and so constructed that the yams stored from one harvest to the next are clearly displayed between the logs which make up the sides (plate 80). To demonstrate the economic importance and the prestige attached to horticultural success, the yam-houses are more carefully constructed than the dwelling-houses, and carry carved and painted barge-boards decorated with mythical fish-birds. The inner plaza is the focus of public life and festivities, and it includes the burial-ground and the dancing-ground – in other words, it is the scene of all ceremonial occasions. This semi-sacred place is the site of the chief's yam-house, and, slightly further from the centre, his dwelling-house. All the inner buildings are hedged about with taboos, especially regarding cooking, which is thought to be inimical to the stored yams. Cooking may only take place in the 'profane' outer ring, the street between the two circles being the theatre of domestic life. All the structures face the central area. The smallest buildings in the village are the 'utility' yam-houses (*sokwaypa*), used for storing seed and personal provisions (plate 77), but also on occasion by adolescents for sleeping in or taking their first lovers. Older Trobrianders may spend some time before marriage in bachelor huts (*bukumatula*) where they may take a succession of lovers to spend the night, while preserving decorum before society. Only if the couple were seen eating together before marriage would offence be caused – this and not sex being the important feature in the definition of Trobriand marriage.

The South Seas have fed many myths in European society since the time of first contact. Bougainville's description of Tahitian

78. (*Above left*) A house interior, Fiji. Linguistic and other cultural attributes link these islands with Melanesia, although house types and the sophistication of *tapa* (bark cloth) suggest Polynesian intrusion. In this interior, the *tapa* wall covering is singularly Fijian in its depth of tone and boldness of geometrical decoration.

79. (*Above*) A round house from Pago Pago, Tutuila, Western (American) Samoa. The floor is of crushed coral; the rolled-up mats may be unfurled from the roof to provide shade and utilize breezes. The climatic constraints are at a minimum, yet the Samoan house is generously constructed despite its minimal use as a 'shelter'.

80. Filling the chief's yam-house, Trobriand Islands. The display yam-house, *bwayma*, on the left of the picture, is larger and more decorated than the chief's dwelling-house on the right, in accordance with its importance as the wealth supply of the chief. Bunches of betel nut hang from the balcony of the dwelling-house, and will be used to pay the workers.

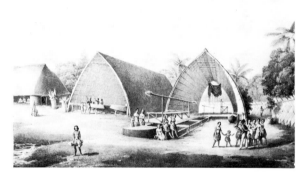

society (although he stayed only ten days on the island) in the great age of 'scientific' exploration was popularized through J.-J. Rousseau's notion of the 'noble savage', and caused a sensation in Europe. The myth of man existing in an Eden or state of nature, carefree, with no suffocating social constraints to bind him, is an attractive one – but in the Polynesian case, at least, this was rather short of the truth. Throughout Polynesia, an individual's position in society was ascribed through genealogy rather than achieved through merit; the more closely one could trace a relationship to the chief, the higher one's rank. There was a belief in *mana* (an immanent power which has been likened to electricity), which was thought to be inherent in all persons and things. People with discrepant amounts of this power (i.e. of different rank) had to be protected from direct contact with each other. The concept of *tabu* formed the corollary of this belief; it accounts for the caste-like division into extremely specialized groups, and with it a high level of technical and aesthetic achievement. Most artistic work was commissioned by the chiefs to enhance their prestige, and the craftsman had to prove and increase the potency of his own and his client's *mana* through his skill. Builders of houses were specialists (*tohungas*) who were organized into guilds, and who would use characteristic patterns of coloured sennit lashings in house construction which, for those who could interpret it, amounted to a 'signature' or hallmark for that guild.

The ceremonial or guest-house of Samoa (plate 79) has undergone an interesting development since the time of European contact. The mild climate means that the need for a 'shelter' hardly exists; nevertheless the original ceremonial house was built to the highest standards and had expansive proportions. The original design was a rectangular plan with apsidal ends, and it was customary for the most honoured chiefs to be disposed at the

81. *(Above left)* This longhouse from Pago Pago, Tutuila, Western Samoa, is a masterpiece of woodwork without nails or screws. This photograph shows the roof supported by king-posts above a post-and-lintel arrangement inside the house. The roof edge is supported by separate posts shaped and lashed to the ring of purlins by sennit cord.

82. *(Above)* A view of the main square in the village of Bea, Tongatapu, in the Tonga Islands; from Dumont D'Urville's *Voyage of the Astrolabe*.

84. *(Above)* A fête given by Toubau, king of Tonga, to Bruni d'Entrecasteaux on his voyage of 1791. The explorer is being received by the court in the elliptical ceremonial house; note the variety of built forms.

85. *(Above right)* An intricately carved Maori foodstore, Rotorua, New Zealand. Warfare and food were the two most important concerns of the traditional Maori society. The elevated storehouses, *pataka*, were often raised on tall posts to protect the contents from damp and vermin. Dwelling-houses were not used to store personal property, so the *pataka* housed clothes, ornaments, tools and weapons as well as preserved foods.

83. *(Left)* The interior of a Maori meeting-house, Rongo Pai, North Island of New Zealand. Ancestors with clubs are depicted on the house posts; the roof panels exhibit the distinctive style of decoration known as 'Gisborne'. This particular house was constructed for the chief Te Kooti, who died soon after it was built, and the interior remained *tabu* until recent times.

rounded ends. But tracing genealogy through to one particular aristocratic male ancestor gave rise to so-called 'conical clans', where honorific titles proliferated in almost geometric progression. This constant inflation of the titled ranks had an impact on architectural form, as Wingert noted, in that the rounded ends had to be increased at the expense of the sides – hence the historical development from rectangular to oval and from oval to round. The ordinary Samoan village house was also round, the form probably suggested by the ceremonial house.

The most southerly outpost of the Polynesian culture area, more than 1,000 miles southeast of western Polynesia, is New Zealand, the home of the Maori. Before European contact there were three main types of Maori dwellings: the 'council-house' (*whare whakairo*) was the most impressive, with delicately carved wooden panels and coloured raffia decoration (plate 83). Large and small undecorated houses were used simply for sleeping (tools, weapons, ornaments and clothes were banished from the house, and instead kept in the raised storehouse, illustrated in plate 85); temporary hunting-lodges were also built. The Maori meeting-house was beautifully constructed, using cords of flax to measure diagonals and pegs driven in to ensure that the excavation was square at the corners. The huge ridge-pole was supported on centre-poles at front and rear; the rafters were lashed into position on them with notchwork so ingenious that the roof and walls were tightly locked together. The roof was covered with heavy thatch, really suitable for more tropical Polynesian climates. Women made the colourfully plaited reedwork wall panels which alternated with wooden panels carved and painted with mythological forms. The building work, painting and carving were controlled by the various *tohungas*, the experts who because of the fusion of religious and aesthetic sensibilities and roles were also regarded as priests.

Eurasia

The word Eurasia refers to the vast landmass stretching from Europe in the west through Asia Minor and the steppes of Russia to Southeast Asia and China. The climatic and ecological diversity is enormous in a continental landmass which extends above the Arctic Circle and below the Tropic of Cancer, but because of its continuity (not without its physical barriers, of course), it is not unreasonable to consider this region as a whole.

The surprising thing is that, in an area so enormous, only comparatively few 'tribal' peoples have survived into modern times. As recently as ten thousand years ago the whole of mankind lived as tribesmen or hunters, but the discovery and exploitation of domestic grain cultivation around this time in the Near East triggered off a whole series of changes which rapidly swept across east and west and on into Africa. The complex aetiology of these changes in the 'fertile crescent' of Mesopotamia that led to the development of agriculture, the production of reliable sur-pluses, craft specialization, cities, states and literacy, while of great fascination, is not our concern here. It is clear, however, that these ideas had influence, and were rapidly diffused – and those nomadic herdsmen or hunter-gatherers unpersuaded by the example of farming were generally drawn into trading relation-ships and eventually absorbed, or displaced through warfare, by the more successful 'citizens'. Tribal peoples not drawn into the vortex of these dominant cultures were pushed into inaccessible enclaves or out into marginal areas too barren and inhospitable to be profitably colonized. In modern times, industrialization has greatly intensified this trend.

The sole representatives of an independent tribal people in western Europe are the Lapps. The Lapps (who call themselves *Sameh*, 'owners of reindeer'), live in the part of northwest Scandi-navia known as Fennoscandia, but they previously lived further south. Their livelihood derives from keeping reindeer, in herds of 300 or more, and they supplement their diet by hunting and fishing. Although the reindeer are tended communally by *siida* – egalitarian groups of families of up to ninety members – they are owned by family heads, and are generally passed on by ultimogeniture, whereby the youngest son inherits. Although the trend now is to live in timber cabins, the traditional Lapp home is a portable tent which takes two main forms: the simplest is the forked-pole tent (*tjagge-kåhte*), but the most original is the umbrella-like bent-pole tent (*åtnåris-kåhte*) (plate 87) constructed of just two pairs of bent birch poles. In plan, the tent was oval, with a hearth occupying the central place and the most honoured sitting closest to it. Family and non-family sat on the left and right of the entrance respectively.

86. A *mudhif* at sunset. The Madan, or Marsh Arabs, who inhabit the marshlands of the lower Tigris and Euphrates in Iraq, build these extraordinary houses from one material only – giant reed (*fragmites communis*). The ribbed arches are constructed of bundles of reeds; split-reed mats clothe the vaulted roof. Plate 7 is an aerial view from the same area.

 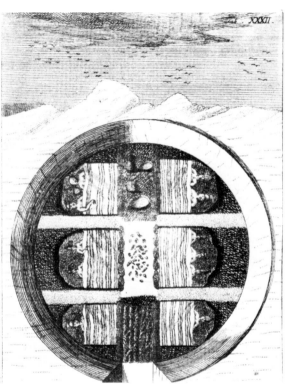

The Lapps used to practise a shamanistic religion, and a small shrine with its own door was previously situated at the back of the tent, where the headman kept a divination drum and offered prayers.

An exotic variant of the portable (in fact, mobile) dwelling is the 'sleigh house' of the nomadic shepherds of the Balkans. These unlikely vehicles were once common from Hungary through Bulgaria to Greece (they are still to be found among the Vlachs of Macedonia); pulled by oxen, these capacious cabins on runners traverse both snow and meadows.

The people of the steppe region of south Siberia — the Kazak, Kirghiz, Kalmuk and Buryat Mongols — are also pastoralists, herding sheep, cattle or camels, and are all celebrated horsemen. Common to them all is the use of the distinctive and very wide-spread domed felt tent, usually known as a yurt, but more properly called a *ger*. This characteristic of Mongol life has been noted by travellers since Marco Polo in the thirteenth century.

Even today, nearly sixty years after the Mongolian revolution of 1921, most of the Buryat population cling to the *ger* as a way of life. The tent itself has changed little externally since those first descriptions. This is perhaps because the domed tent is ideally

87. A curved pole tent of the Lapps, reindeer herders from Northern Scandinavia. The second engraving (from Knud Leems' *Finmartens Lapp*, published in 1767) shows a schematic — and possibly fanciful — sleeping arrangement.

adapted to steppe nomadism and can be set up or struck by a small team in thirty minutes. The *ger* (plate 88) is constructed with several expanded lattices forming a circular wall which meets a post-and-lintel doorway. Willow rods, connected to a heavy wooden hoop which forms the apex of the roof, are tied to the framework. As many large pieces of felt as are needed to keep out the cold are wrapped around the walls and over the roof and fastened with horsehair rope. The central hoop was previously left uncovered to provide a smoke-hole, but the Buryat now have efficient stoves with pipes to take the smoke clear. Woollen rugs may cover the floor, or be hung around the walls or over the framework before the fleece felts go on, to make the interior more colourful.

There must be a high degree of organization of this restricted space for life to be comfortable. Among the Mongols, people and objects are allotted carefully designated spaces within their tents, and these social designations have changed only in detail from the thirteenth century to the twentieth, and from Tartary to Mongolia. Briefly, the floor area of the Buryat tent is thought of as divided into four sectors. The southern portion from the door to the hearth was the junior or low-status half; from behind the hearth to the back of the tent was the high-status section, the *xoimor*. This division was complemented by a separation into male (ritually pure) and female (ritually impure) halves, on the west and east respectively. Male visitors would therefore keep to the SW sector, women visitors to the SE, the hostess, her children and kin would receive them in the NE, and the seat of honour for the host and high-status guests would be in the NW sector. Objects would be categorized in the same way: household utensils would be kept in the 'female' half, valuables and hunting equipment in the 'male' half. At the northernmost perimeter of the *xoimor* would be a Buddhist altar (the Buryats followed a shamanist Lamaist version of Buddhism). Since the 1921 revolution, however, there have been fundamental changes in this rigid categorization of space – a children's bed may now be found in the place previously reserved for the altar, the honorific apogee of the old hierarchic system. The location of objects and people in the present-day tent now tends to show the visitor how 'progressive' the family is, which can be measured by the degree of divergence from the 'old order'.

In the densely populated southeast culture area, which includes India, Southeast Asia and Indonesia, tribal people survive relatively unchanged only in ethnic enclaves; most of the inhabitants are nominally Muslim or Hindu, live as peasant farmers, and belong in some way to national cultures. One example of the result of geographical isolation aiding the survival of an autonomous

88. Felt *gers* of the Buryat Mongols from the Mongolian People's Republic. Extra layers of felt may be added as insulation against the harsh steppe winters. The form of this portable house has changed little since the thirteenth century, to judge from travellers' descriptions.

89. Summer huts from the Kamchatka peninsula, northeast Siberia, with drying racks for skins. The drawing is by John Webber, a member of James Cook's expedition of 1779.

90. The extraordinary 'morung' or *deka chang* of the Ao Nagas from the Naga Hills of Assam – a photograph taken in 1903. It is both a club-house and a guard-house, women being excluded. The tiny doors at front and rear had a defensive function, protecting the warriors from surprise intrusions. This 'closed' type of morung was typical of the western villagers of Nagaland. *(See also plate 92)*

91. House-building in Assam, northern India. This illustrates the building of a tribal house as a community enterprise. An operation of this scale requires the mobilization of ties of kinship and friendship, and will incur debts the repayment of which will be extended throughout the local group for some time to come.

culture — at least up to colonial times — is provided by the Toda tribe of southern India. The Toda live in the Nilgiri Hills, a high undulating plateau, cut off from the lowland around them by steep cliffs at the foot of which are dense forests formerly rife with malaria. Up on the 6,000-foot plateau, however, the tropical climate of southern India is greatly moderated. The Toda devote most of their time to their herds of buffalo; they neither hunt, fish, nor plant crops. Their rudimentary material culture is produced by neighbouring tribes such as the artisan Kota, and grain is obtained by tribute or purchase from the Badaga, also neighbours. One of the very few crafts in which individual Toda have become specialists is house-building. Their unusual huts (plate 93) are in the shape of a half-barrel, the frame made from bamboo curved to meet at the top. The thatched roofs extend down the sides to the excavated base, and overhang at the ends to form porches. During the day, women pound grain at the rear, and men churn milk at the front. Anthropologists are more interested in the Toda for their marriage customs than their houses; they are one of the few groups in the ethnographic record (the Kandyans of Sri-Lanka, the Marquesans, and some Tibetan and Himalayan cultures are others) where a wife is co-married to two or more husbands. The Toda variety is called fraternal polyandry, because brothers share their wife — indeed there may also be more than one wife.

92. The front of an Assamese 'morung' of the eastern type. The roof slopes down towards the back, though not in such an exaggerated way as the closed type from the west. The deep porch here conceals the main pillars, carved with heads, hornbills, tigers and elephants. *(See also plate 90)*

Much further east are the richly diverse cultures of Indonesia and insular Southeast Asia. In highland Sumatra, the Batak, Minangkabau (whose name means 'victorious buffalo') and Rejang are well-known as remarkably accomplished builders. The traditional Toba Batak house (plate 94 shows a street of such houses) was raised on piles, entry being gained by a trap-door in the floor. Roofs were high and saddle-backed, projecting from either end (plate 96) — a common Indonesian feature which, it has been suggested, derives its shape from a ship's bow and stern, a reminder of a distant maritime past; but this explanation seems to be rather far-fetched.

At the far eastern end of this culture area, in a zone between the Oriental and Australasian faunal regions, live the Toradja, on the island of Sulawesi (Celebes). Toradja life revolves around the cult of their dead, the celebration of their water-buffalo, and the decoration of their quite magnificent houses and rice-stores. Villages were previously built on hill-tops because they believe their first ancestor descended there; now they may be found on terraced slopes, with ten or more houses arranged in a straight line. If it were not for the majestic peaked roofs at the front and rear, the houses would be all but hidden by the gardens of bamboo, sugar palms and coconut trees. Again, the houses are raised on piles, and most have verandahs, but the most striking features are the beautifully decorated panels of the overhanging gable ends. These panels have richly complex geometrical designs in various harmonious hues of ochre, and stylized representations of a long-necked bird. The omnipresent water-buffalo decorates the front of the house in the form of a carved and painted buffalo-head, and a collection of the same animal's horns, a tally of the number sacrificed, is attached to the pole which supports the gable. These *tongkonan* (houses founded by an ancestor, and consecrated with sacrificial pigs) are thought to represent the cosmos — the northern part is the most sacred, the roof is the sky.

Can we draw lessons from these widely dispersed examples of tribal houses? As Socrates observed, 'The city without is built on the city within'; how much more true this is of these communities, with their clear notions of style and way of life, than it is of our own. The suitability of the built environment is hourly put to the test, and this brings home to us that architecture is the most practical of arts, constrained as it is by problems of utility that do not apply to the others: the structure must stand before it can speak. This refining process has left us with a diverse global heritage; its riches can now be shared to our pleasure and our profit.

93. A Toda hut from the Nilgiri Hills of South India. The hut is semi-excavated, with a raised earth seat on each side of the small door. The roof is carefully thatched in layers; note the way in which the parabolic end arch is laced. Toda 'dairy temples' are identical in form to these dwellings, despite their different function.

94. *(Left)* A Batak village in north-central Sumatra. The Batak, along with the Minangkabau and Redjang, are celebrated builders from Indonesia; their *huta* (villages) consist of six to ten closely built multi-family houses.

96. *(Right)* Detail of the huge saddle-back roof of a typical Batak house. Ceremonial drums can be seen below the gable end. The carved decorations attached to the main posts generally represent buffalo horns.

95. *(Below)* Part of Ináka village on the east coast of Camorta Island, Nicobar Islands, photographed in 1907. These finely constructed houses, one of which is some way from completion, demonstrate the diversity of form even within a small-scale community, with the happy co-existence of domed and gabled pile dwellings.

Bibliography

General Anthropology
Forde, C. Daryll: *Habitat, economy and society.* Methuen, London, 1934
Sahlins, Marshall: *Tribesmen.* Prentice-Hall, Englewood Cliffs, New Jersey, 1968
Snow, Dean: *The American Indians.* Thames & Hudson, London, 1976

Visual and Theoretical Approaches to Tribal Architecture
Fraser, D.: *Village Planning in the Primitive World.* Braziller, London and New York, 1968
Gerster, Georg: *Grand Design: the earth from above.* Paddington Press, London, 1976
Hall, Edward T.: *The hidden dimension.* Doubleday, Garden City, New York, 1966
Oliver, Paul: *Shelter and Society.* Barrie & Jenkins, London, 1969
Rapoport, Amos: *House, Form and Culture.* Prentice-Hall, Englewood Cliffs, New Jersey, 1969
Rudofsky, Bernard: *Architecture without architects.* Museum of Modern Art, New York, 1964
Rudofsky, Bernard: *The prodigious builders.* Secker & Warburg, London, 1977
Wingert, Paul S.: *Primitive art: its traditions and styles.* OUP, New York, 1962
Ucko, Peter J. et al: *Man, settlement and urbanism.* Duckworth, London, 1972

Area Studies of Tribal Architecture
Denyer, Susan: *African Traditional Architecture.* Heinemann Educational, London, 1978
Fernea, Robert A., Gerster, Georg: *Nubians in Egypt.* University of Texas, Austin, 1973
Forge, Anthony: 'Learning to see in New Guinea', in *Socialization, the approach from Social Anthropology* (ed. Philip Mayer). Tavistock Publications, London, 1970
Humphrey, Caroline: *Inside a Mongolian tent.* New Society, London, 31 October 1974
Morgan, Lewis H.: *House and house life of the American aborigines* (1881). Chicago U.P., Chicago, republished 1965
Oliver, Paul: *Shelter in Africa.* Barrie & Jenkins, London, 1971
Prussin, Labelle: *Architecture in northern Ghana.* University of California Press, Berkeley and Los Angeles, 1969
Spini, Tito and Spini, Sandro: *Togu na: Casa della parola, struttura di socializzazione della comunità Dogon.* Electa, Milan, 1976

Ethnographies and Travel Accounts
Cranstone, B. A. L.: *Melanesia: a short ethnography.* Trustees of the British Museum, London, 1961
Gide, André: *Travels in the Congo.* Knopf, New York, 1929
Griaule, Marcel: *Conversations with Ogotemmêli.* O.U.P. for International African Institute, 1965
Malinowski, Bronislaw: *The sexual life of savages.* Routledge, London, 1929
The travels of Marco Polo the Venetian. Everyman Library, Dent, London, 1908

Acknowledgements and list of illustrations

The author and Blacker Calmann Cooper Ltd would like to thank the museums who allowed works in their collections to be reproduced in this book. They would also like to thank the photographers and photographic agencies who allowed their photographs to be reproduced.

1. House of the Yukpa Indians. Photo Paul Henley
2. Painting of a sacred house at Dorey, New Guinea. Courtesy of the Trustees of the British Museum, London
3. East Anatolian village. Photo Denis McGilvray
4. An Australian bark shelter. Photo Axel Poignant
5. Iban longhouse at Sarawak on Kalimantan (Borneo). Photo Haddon Coll., Cambridge
6. Dogon compound. Photo Werner Forman Archive
7. Madan settlement in Iraq. Photo Georg Gerster (John Hillelson Agency)
8. Unfinished *Dawi* from the Purari delta region of New Guinea. Photo Haddon Coll., Cambridge
9. Meidob house in the Sudan. Photo Elizabeth Hales
10. Decorated Nubian house in southern Egypt. Photo Georg Gerster (John Hillelson Agency)
11. An Annamese village near Hanoi, Vietnam. Photo Werner Forman Archive
12. Cult house from the Sepik River, New Guinea. Photo Anthony Forge
13. Songhai village in Mali. Photo Georg Gerster (John Hillelson Agency)
14. Conical house in Panare territory, Venezuela. Photo Paul Henley
15. Millet granaries from Fadiout, coastal Senegal. Photo Daily Telegraph Colour Library
16. Bedouin tent from Qatar in the Arabian Gulf. Photo Shelagh Weir
17. Fortified house in Afghanistan. Photo Denis McGilvray
18. Market town in the Barat region of Yemen. Photo F. Veranda
19. Houses from the Barat region of Yemen. Photo F. Veranda
20. Paintings on a house of the Kenuzi Nubians. Photo Georg Gerster (John Hillelson Agency)
21. Zulu kraal from Natal, South Africa. Photo Clive Hicks
22. Hut of the Ngwame Bantu. Photo Werner E. Kauffel. Film Akademische Druck-u. Verlagsanstatt, Graz
23. Village of pile dwellings on Lake Nokwé, Benin. Photo Georg Gerster (John Hillelson Agency)
24. Oasis town of El Oued in the Souf region of the Algerian Sahara. Photo Georg Gerster (John Hillelson Agency)
25. Goatskin tent of the Tuareg of northern Upper Volta. Photo Robert Hecht
26. Fulani dwelling in northern Upper Volta. Photo Robert Hecht
27. Logone-Birni in the Cameroun. Photo Griaule (Musée de l'Homme, Paris)
28. Fulani village in northern Upper Volta. Photo Robert Hecht
29. Songhai tents near Timbuctu, Mali. Photo Georg Gerster (John Hillelson Agency)
30. Dogon village near Banani, Mali. Photo Griaule (Musée de l'Homme, Paris)
31. Dogon village from the Bandiagara escarpment in Mali. Photo Werner Forman Archive
32. Dogon *togu na* at Banani, Mali. Photo Tito Spini
33. Dogon *togu na* at Banani, Mali. Photo Tito Spini
34. Maasai dwellings from Ngorongoro, Tanzania. Photo M. Satchwell
35. Hutu hut from Rwanda. Photo Shelagh Weir
36. Building a Sherbro house on the coast of Sierra Leone. Photo Carol MacCormack
37. Mousgoum houses of northern Cameroun. Photo Musée de l'Homme, Paris
38. Dogon *togu na* from Madougou, Mali. Photo Tito Spini
39. Orma Galla village of Kenya. Photo R. L. Matthews (Daily Telegraph Colour Library)
40. Labwor round-hut from Uganda. Photo Dr Ray Abrahams

41. Hausa compound wall in northern Nigeria. Photo Robert Pokrant
42. House in Djenne, Mali. Photo Werner Forman Archive
43. The town of Buso in southern Ethiopia. Photo Georg Gerster (John Hillelson Agency)
44. Hausa house from Kano, northern Nigeria. Photo Marion Barnett
45. 'Modern' Hausa house from Kano, northern Nigeria. Photo Marion Barnett
46. House of the chief of the Bushongo Kuba, from Kasai in central Zaire. Musée Royale d'Afrique, Tervueren
47. Houses of the Manga of Zaire. Photo Haddon Coll., Cambridge
48. Barasana man decorating a longhouse. Photo Georg Gerster (John Hillelson Agency)
49. Ojibwa tent from Canada. Photo Haddon Coll., Cambridge
50. Igloo from the Lindstrom valley. Photo Royal Geographical Society
51. Earth lodges of the Californian Indians in the Sacramento valley
52. Settlement near Lake Huron, painted by John Kane. Art Gallery of Ontario, Toronto
53. Tlingit chief's house in Cape Fox, Alaska. Museum of the American Indian, New York
54. Pawnee earth lodge. Photo Haddon Coll., Cambridge
55. Earth lodges of the Mandan Indians. American Museum of Natural History, New York
56. The village of Secotan in Virginia, painted by John Wyth. Courtesy of the Trustees of the British Museum, London
57. 'Cliff palace' in the Mesa Verde National Park in Colorado. Photo Werner Forman Archive
58. Tepee of the Blackfoot Indians from Montana. Photo Haddon Coll., Cambridge
59. Amazonian village. Photo Mosely
60. Mayan Indian house in Belize. Photo J. C. H. King
61. War gathering of Witoto Indians outside their communal house. Photo Haddon Coll., Cambridge
62. Barasana longhouse undergoing decoration. Photo Brian Moser (Allan and Sarah Hutchison Agency)
63. Yagua dwelling in Peru. Photo Nicholas Guppy (Daily Telegraph Colour Library)
64. Dwellings of Tierra del Fuego by Sydney Parkinson. Courtesy of the Trustees of the British Museum, London
65. Chimbu village in the eastern highlands of Papua-New Guinea. Photo Axel Poignant
66. Buildings of Likiliki, New Ireland. Courtesy of the Trustees of the British Museum, London
67. Courthouse of the Solomon Islands. Photo Haddon Coll., Cambridge
68. Village scene on Siar island, New Guinea. Photo Haddon Coll., Cambridge
69. Bachelors' house in Humboldt Bay, Irian Jaya (West New Guinea). Photo Haddon Coll., Cambridge
70. Chimbu women's house in the eastern highlands of Papua-New Guinea. Photo Axel Poignant
71. Houses in the Papuan Gulf. Courtesy of the Trustees of the British Museum, London
72. Men's club-house from the Purari Delta, New Guinea. Photo Haddon Coll., Cambridge
73. Men's ceremonial house from the Middle Sepik river, Papua-New Guinea. Photo Axel Poignant
74. Haus tambaran in north Abelam, Papua-New Guinea. Photo Anthony Forge
75. Interior of Sepik River meeting-house. Photo Axel Poignant
76. Chief's house in the Trobriand Islands. Photo J. W. Leach
77. Chief's yam-house in the Trobriand Islands. Photo J. W. Leach
78. House interior on Fiji. Photo Haddon Coll., Cambridge
79. Round house from Pago Pago, Western Samoa. Photo Haddon Coll., Cambridge
80. Filling the chief's yam-house in the Trobriand Islands. Photo J. W. Leach
81. Longhouse from Pago Pago, Western Samoa. Photo Haddon Coll., Cambridge
82. Main square of Bea in the Tonga islands. Courtesy of the Trustees of the British Museum, London
83. Interior of a Maori meeting-house in the North Island of New Zealand. Photo Axel Poignant
84. Fête given by the king of Tonga. Courtesy of the Trustees of the British Museum, London
85. Maori foodstore in Rotorua. Photo Axel Poignant
86. Marsh Arab mudhif. Photo Nik Wheeler (Black Star Agency)
87. Lapp tent. Courtesy of the Trustees of the British Museum, London
88. Felt gers of the Buryat Mongols. Photo Dr Caroline Humphrey
89. Kamchatka summer huts. Courtesy of the Trustees of the British Museum, London
90. 'Morung' of the Ao Nagas of Assam. Photo Haddon Coll., Cambridge
91. House-building in Assam. Photo Haddon Coll., Cambridge
92. 'Morung' from Assam. Photo Haddon Coll., Cambridge
93. Toda hut from the Nilgiri Hills of South India. Photo Haddon Coll., Cambridge
94. Batak village in Sumatra. Photo Werner Forman Archive
95. Ináka village in the Nicobar Islands. Photo Haddon Coll., Cambridge
96. Roof of Batak house in Sumatra. Photo Werner Forman Archive

Diagrams
Fig. 1. Tiv homestead, Nigeria (after Bohannan)
Fig. 2. Plan of a Bororo village, Brazil (after Albisetti)
Fig. 3. Idealized layout of a Dogon village (after Griaule)
Fig. 4. Two-storey Dogon house (after Griaule)
Fig. 5. Plan of a Trobriand village (after Malinowski)

Index

An *italic* number refers to an illustration or caption on that page

Abelam, 72–6; *78*
aborigines, Australian, *8*
aborigines, Tasmanian, 16
Afghanistan, *24*
Africa, 29–51
Alaska, 54, 55; *59*
Algonkians, 62
Amazonia, 10, 22, 65–9; *23, 64*
Ambuti, *78*
Americas, 53–69
Anatolia, 5
Annamese, 13; *15*
Ao Nagas, *89*

Aola Bay, *72*
Arabs, 30–2
Arikara, *59*
Assam, *89*
Atakora, 44
Australia, 69; *8*
Azanians, 50
Aztec, 63

Badaga, 90
Bantu, *30*
Barasana, 67–9; *52, 66*
Barat, 25
Batak, 13, 91; *92, 93*
Bea, *82*
Bedouin, *24*

Belize, 65
Bellacoola, 55
Benin, 44; *31*
Berbers, 30–2
Blackfoot, 10; *62*
Bororo, 22; *23*
Brazil, 69; *64*
British Columbia, 55
Buryat, 5, 10, 86–7; *88*
Bushongo Kuba, *50*
Buso, 48; *48*

Cameroun, *36, 44*
Canada, 53, 56
Cape Fox, 58
Caribou Inuit, 54

Çatal Hüyük, 5; *7*
Chad, 32
Chimbu, 71; *70*
Chugach, 54
Colombia, 67; *52, 61, 66*
Colorado, *60*
Cuzco, 63

Dakota Indians, 62
Dirima, *70*
Djenne, 50; *47*
Doab Road, *24*
Dogon, 10, 36–44; *10, 38–41, 45*
Doreri, *75*
Dorey, *6*

Egypt, 32; *14*
Engaruku, 50
Erzurum, *7*
Eskimos, 53–5
Ethiopia, 5, 48; *48*
Eurasia, 85–93

Fadiout, *21*
Felombaga, *36*
Fiji, *80*
Fulani, 32–6; *35, 36*

Gallinomero, 55
Gao, 50
Ghana, 50
Greenland, 54
Guadalcanal, *72*
Gumine, 71; *70*

Haida, 55
Hausa, 36, 51; *47, 49*
Hidatsa, 59
Huron, Lake, 56
Hutu, *43*

Iatmul, *77*
Iban, 9–10; *9*
Ináka, *92*
Incas, 63
India, 90; *89*
Indians, American, 16, 53, 55–69; *55–62*
Indonesia, 92, 93
Inuit, 53–5
Iraq, *11, 84*
Irian Jaya, *73*
Iroquois, 62–3

Kakaway, 51
Kalimantan, 9
Kalmuk, 86
Kamari, *75*
Kamchatka, *88*
Kandyans, 90
Kanganaman, *77*
Kano, 50, 51; *49*
Kazak, 86
Kenuzi, *28*
Kenya, 45; *46*
Kinbanggwa, *78*
Kirghiz, 86
Konso, *48*
Kota, 90
Koumbi-Saleh, 48–50
Kwakiutl, 55

Labbézanga, *19*

Labwor, *46*
Lapps, 85–6; *86*
Likiliki, *71*
Logone-Birni, *36*

Maasai, 45–6; *42*
Macedonia, 86
Madan, *11, 84*
Madougou, *45*
Mali, 18, 36; *19, 37–41, 45, 47*
Mandan, 59; *59*
Manga, *51*
Maori, 83; *82, 83*
Maprik, *17*
Marquesans, 90
Massa, 5
Massim, 76
Matma, 32
Mato Grosso, *23*
Maya, 63; *65*
Meidob, 13; *14*
Melanesia, 71–80
Mesa Verde, *60*
Minangkabau, 91; *92*
Mongols, 5, 10, 86–7; *88*
Montagnais, 62
Montana, *62*
Mousgoum, *44*
Mundurucu, 69
Mushenge, *50*

Nalya, *51*
New Guinea, 13, 16, 71–6; *6, 12, 73*
New Ireland, *71*
New Mexico, 55
New York State, 62
New Zealand, 83; *82, 83*
Ngelima, *51*
Ngorongoro, *42*
Ngwame Bantu, *30*
Nicobar Islands, *92*
Nigeria, 22, 51; *22, 47, 49*
Nilgiri Hills, 90
Nokwé, Lake, *31*
North Vietnam, *15*
Nubians, 13; *14, 28*

Oceania, 71–83
Ojibwa, *53*
Omarakana, 76–80; *76, 79*
Ona, 69
Orma Galla, *46*
Ottawa Indians, 62; *56*
El Oued, *33*

Pago Pago, *80, 82*
Panare, 18, 65–7; *20*
Panga, *51*
Papua-New Guinea, *17, 70, 74–5, 77–8*
Pawnee, 59; *58*
Peru, 63, 69; *67*
Plains Indians, 59
Point Barrow, 54
Polynesia, 71, 82–3
Powhatan, 62–3
Pueblo Indians, 55, 63; *60*

Qatar, *16*

Redjang, 91; *92*
Rongo Pai, *82*
Rwanda, *43*

Sacramento Valley, 55
Sacsahuamán, 63
Sahara, 29–32
Samoa, 82–3; *80, 82*
San Estevan, *65*
Sanga, *38*
Sarawak, *9*
Secotan, 63; *57*
Senegal, 32; *21*
Sepik, 76
Shenge, *44*
Sherbro, *44*
Siar Island, *73*
Siberia, 53, 54, 86; *88*
Sierra Leone, *44*
Siwan, 32
Sokoto, 51
Solomon Islands, 72; *72*
Somba, 44
Songhai, 18; *19, 37*
Southeast Asia, 69
Soweto, 16
Ssola, 44
Sudan, 44; *14*
Sulawesi, 91
Sumatra, 91; *92*
Suq al 'Ainau, *25*

Tabadi, *73*
Tahiti, 80–2
Tambernu, 44
Tanzania, 45, 50; *42*
Tareumiut, 54
Tasmania, 16
Tierra del Fuego, 16, 69; *68*
Timbuctu, 50
Tiv, 18; *22*
Tlingit, 55; *58*
Toda, 90
Togo, 44
Tonga, *82, 83*
Tongatapu, *82*
Toradja, 91
Trobriand Islands, 76–80; *21, 76, 79, 81*
Tuareg, 18, 30–2; *34*
Tunisia, 32
Turkey, *7*
Tutsi, *43*
Tutuila, *80, 82*
Twa, *43*

Uganda, 46
Upper Volta, 44; *34, 35, 36*

Vaupes, 67
Venezuela, 18, 65–7; *6, 20*
Virginia, *57*
Vlachs, 86

Walata, 50
West Africa, 18
Witoto, *61, 66*

Yagua, 69; *67*
Yemen, 44; *25*
Yukpa, 5; *6*

Zaire, *50, 51*
Zaria, 51
Zimbabwe, 50
Zuñi, 63